# The Roots of Lesbian & Gay Oppression

**A MARXIST VIEW**

# The Roots of Lesbian & Gay Oppression

## A Marxist View

WW Publishers

**Library of Congress Cataloging in Publication Data**

McCubbin, Bob
   The roots of lesbian and gay oppression.

   1. Gay liberation movement.   2. Homosexuality–
History.  I. Title.
HQ76.5.M3     301.41'57       78-24587
ISBN 0-89567-116-6

Original title: The Gay Question: A Marxist Appraisal
First edition March 1976
Second edition July 1979
Third edition April 1993

Copyright © 1976 by World View Publishers
Preface and Afterword Copyright © 1993 by WW Publishers

WW Publishers
55 West 17 Street, New York, NY 10011

## Contents

Preface ............................................. VII
Introduction ........................................ XV
Homosexuality in Primitive Society ............... 1
The Overthrow of the Matriarchy
and Early Class Society ............................ 9
The Evolution of Patriarchal Religion ............ 17
The Rise of Christianity and Medieval Europe .... 23
Lesbian and Gay Oppression Under Capitalism .... 33
Communism vs. Fascism: Two Lines on
Lesbians and Gays .................................. 43
Selected Photos of Lesbian and Gay History ...... 53
Lesbian and Gay Oppression in the U.S. .......... 69
The Struggle that will End
Lesbian and Gay Oppression ....................... 79
Afterword ........................................... 87
Author's Note ....................................... 97
Selected Bibliography ............................... 99

## ABOUT THE AUTHOR

Bob McCubbin is a teacher, writer and activist. He joined Workers World Party in 1967 and was a founder of WWP's Lesbian, Gay and Transgender Caucus. He has long been active in the struggle for justice in New York and in California, where he now lives.

# PREFACE

This book was originally published as *The Gay Question* in 1976, during the first flush of the modern lesbian and gay liberation movement. The 1969 Stonewall Rebellion had galvanized a generation of gay men, lesbians, and transsexuals, transvestites and other transgendered people. It was a time of ferment, of questioning. Around the country, people were on the march. The epochal struggles of oppressed nationalities inside the U.S. were expressed through groups like the Black Panther Party, the Young Lords, La Raza Unida, the American Indian Movement and I Wor Kun. They fought for self-determination as colonized peoples within an imperialist country built on profound, institutionalized racism. The great civil rights movement also led to the battle to stop the war in Vietnam, and to the women's movement. Young people were inspired by liberation struggles in Africa, Asia and Latin America, and disillusioned and alienated by capitalist society that seemed to thrive on war, misery and exploitation.

People sought new approaches, new ideas. Many looked to revolutionaries like Mao Zedong, Fidel Castro, Chiang Ching, Che Guevara, Lolita Lebron, Angela Davis, Erika Huggins and Malcolm X. They turned to the writings of Karl Marx, Frederick Engels and V.I. Lenin. A whole generation of the working class and the oppressed communities, along with a great many middle-class students and youths, was ready to reject old ways and tired ideas, to challenge the status quo of racism, sexism—*and* lesbian/gay oppression.

That was the period in which this book was written and first published. Bob McCubbin, like many other young gay radicals, was already a veteran of the struggles of the era. Like others, he was eager to now link the lesbian and gay struggle with all the other great movements for social justice.

It was crucial to break down the barriers that isolated the gay community and blocked the development of gay-straight unity and solidarity. But unity—so necessary to the struggle of workers and oppressed peoples against the ruling class—would be hard to build as long as the old ideas held sway.

This is a contest for people's hearts and minds, an effort to break the grip of centuries of lies. This is combat over consciousness, which is in many ways the most difficult terrain of all. McCubbin recognized that. Ultimately, the purpose of this book was—and is—to raise consciousness and help sweep away all the rotten junk, all the bigotry and prejudices accumulated at so much cost to humankind.

In the years since this book was written, gay people, many of them now open and proud about their sexual identity, have fought side by side with straights on many issues—against apartheid and U.S. intervention in Central America, in strikes and union organizing drives, for child care and against cutbacks. The work force has grown more multinational, more diverse, with women and people of color for the first time composing the majority. The terrible AIDS crisis has taken a monstrous toll in the gay community and hit Black and Latino gays and straights in disproportionate numbers. All these objective factors affected people's lives and thus their subjective experience. As a result of the living struggle and the altered social landscape, support for and solidarity with the lesbian and gay community has deepened and broadened in the quarter century after Stonewall.

Anti-gay attitudes hinder humanity's progress. But they haven't just withered away and disappeared. They couldn't. Homophobia is too deep, too entrenched. The ruling class relies too much on lesbian/gay oppression as a key device to sow division and block effective resistance from the working class, much as it uses racism as its constant, basic instrument. The powers that be have used every tool at their disposal—in particular, their control of the media, education, and the legal system—to maintain and enforce fear and hatred of gays, lesbians, and transvestites, transsexuals and other transgendered people. In every year since this book was first published, the lesbian and gay community has had to fight this ongoing onslaught—from the Anita Bryant-led anti-gay referendum campaigns of the 1970s to AIDS-related discrimination in the

1980s to the Pentagon's heightened anti-gay offensive in the 1990s.

Nevertheless, the nearly overwhelming anti-gay monolith, erected and continuously buttressed by class society, is starting to crumble. This book contributed to that. It is a battering ram that hit, and still hits, hard. Its unparalleled achievement was to offer a historical analysis of the development of lesbian and gay oppression—and through this glimpse of what came before, an inspiring, empowering vision of what can come next.

That achievement still stands. With all that has happened since— the growth of the movement, new alliances and coalitions, victories and setbacks, the AIDS crisis—Bob McCubbin's contribution to understanding the roots of oppression is just as relevant today as in 1976.

In this one slim volume, McCubbin manages to take in the broad sweep of human history. He examines the current state of lesbian and gay oppression in the context of many milennia of social development. It's a potentially perilous undertaking; the result could have been a dry academic treatise of marginal esoteric interest but no practical value.

Instead, McCubbin accomplishes something wonderful: a work that, although scholarly, is a really good read. That's important, because this book was never meant to moulder on library shelves. These pages are ammunition. Their purpose is to arm lesbians, gays and transgendered people with the knowledge that life does not have to be lived as we now know it—a life of oppression, persecution and discrimination, no civil rights; a constant struggle to maintain pride in our identity despite overwhelming social pressure to the contrary. The purpose is also to inform, enlighten and arm straight people, and build solidarity.

These pages contain the startling information that life was not always like this. Homophobia is not natural. In fact, homophobia is an artificial construct and a relatively recent one at that. It's lesbian and gay oppression that is an aberration—not lesbians and gays.

This is vital news. And there's more. Once we understand that homosexuality has always been a natural form of human expression, McCubbin takes the next step. He shows us how, when, and especially why everything got so twisted around that gays, lesbians and transgendered people—once accepted and in some cultures even honored—became ostracized as pariahs and driven deep into suffocating closets whose doors stayed closed for many centuries. He identifies the culprit: class society in its modern form, the capitalist system.

From there, it's not much of a leap to recognizing the way out of this mess.

▼

The state of research has not, of course, remained static in the years since McCubbin wrote this book. Historians, anthropologists, and others have continued to delve into many of the questions addressed here. Women's Studies and then Lesbian and Gay Studies emerged as academic disciplines. And here's the remarkable thing: The current scholarship utterly confirms the analysis presented here. So this book isn't just written in a fresh style—the facts remain fresh, the thesis firmly rooted in reality as confirmed by the latest evidence.

Bourgeois ideologists would dispute that. The observations in the Introduction about the class bias of supposedly impartial commentators still hold true. The other side well understands the power of ideas and knowledge. That explains the vicious attacks against the acclaimed archaeologist Professor Marija Gimbutas of the University of California at Los Angeles. In her books *The Language of the Goddess* and *The Civilization of the Goddess* Gimbutas presents concrete proof that matriarchal cultures organized on a primitive communist basis preceded the patriarchy and the establishment of social/economic classes. Further, Gimbutas shows that these societies were much as McCubbin portrays them: communal, cooperative, the antithesis of the racist, sexist, anti-gay culture in which we now live. For challenging the academic establishment by daring to assert that it wasn't always like this, Gimbutas has been called a charlatan, a fraud and worse.

In fact, she is just one of many whose work (even if they themselves don't realize it) leads to the inevitable conclusion that if it wasn't always like this, it doesn't always have to stay this way. The book *Living the Spirit,* compiled by Gay American Indians, examines the rich variety of sexual expression in some pre-class societies. So from Lewis Morgan and Frederick Engels in the 19th century and Margaret Mead earlier in the 20th, and from contemporary researchers like Gimbutas and G.A.I., an unbroken trail of evidence leads here, to these pages.

For the scientific facts in all their exhaustive details, the reader should turn to the original sources. But for the essence, distilled and interpreted for the unabashed purpose of aiding the lesbian and gay struggle, you need seek no further than this book.

Much has changed since 1975. New developments spurred the struggle forward. A different political climate molded a new generation of gay, lesbian and transgender activists. Today's angry young radicals came of age not during a period of protests and upheaval, but in an era of cutbacks, attacks on affirmative action, an upsurge in racist violence, imperialist interventions. They came out in the time of AIDS and the concurrent rise in anti-gay attacks.

They could have retreated into a purely defensive posture in the face of political reaction and medical tragedy. That didn't happen. Instead, they grew angrier, more defiant—and more numerous. Groups like the Gay Liberation Front disappeared, but the new generation created formations like ACT UP and Queer Nation and Lesbian Avengers and Transgender Nation. Young militants gravitate to these organizations because of their fighting spirit and in-your-face refusal to kowtow to homophobic norms and conventions.

The community's response to AIDS, in particular, has been heroic. Lesbian and gay people have cared for the ill in the face of brutal government neglect—and at the same time demanded an end to the neglect in an energetic movement that affirms the beautiful gay spark of life even in the face of so much death.

At the same time, a new but related movement has begun to emerge. Today, a transgender community composed of a wide range of gender expression and sexual orientation is coalescing into a fight-back movement. While many people think of the lesbian/gay and transgender populations as one and the same, these two groupings actually only partially overlap; the majority of transgendered people are straight or bisexual. But the struggle for gender freedom has enormous importance for the lesbian and gay community. Transgendered lesbians and gay men have been on the front lines of forging the resistance to lesbian and gay oppression from the time of the homosexual emancipation movement in the early part of this century to the Stonewall Rebellion and beyond.*

McCubbin shows that although gender has been expressed differently in divergent cultures and historical periods, transgender has always been a part of human expression. Gender oppression, on the other hand, has not always existed. This book illuminates how the roots of gender, sexual and national oppression are intertwined with the growth of class society and the communities face a common enemy. Defending gender freedom will serve to strengthen the lesbian and gay community, and build ties with the huge and oppressed transgender community.

For all these fighters who've taken up the struggle in the last two decades, and for all people who stand for liberation and against oppression, this book remains essential reading. It's the stuff of history. It's the stuff of pride. It will make you stronger.

Most important, it will provide you with a theoretical understanding to fuel and direct your anger. Reading this book, you will learn that the roots of lesbian and gay oppression lie buried deep in the fetid soil of class society. Class struggle and ultimately socialist revolution are the means to uproot that oppression once and for all.

Very little in the text has been changed for this new edition. Some language was updated—"gay women," for example, are now "lesbians." The introduction was very slightly revised. But the book itself remains so valuable that, with these minor exceptions, it was left intact.

An afterword has, however, been appended. The passage of time and all that has happened on the world stage since the original publication may make the last chapter somewhat jarring to today's reader. So after the chapter titled "The Struggle That Will End

Lesbian and Gay Oppression" there is a new section, titled "The Struggle Continues." This afterword provides some commentary on the contemporary context.

Finally, Bob McCubbin offers an Author's Note with a modest proposal for how to move the struggle forward.

Here, then, in a new edition: a clear, dispassionate, yet utterly partisan review of a history of pain, persecution, courage and pride. You have in your hands a powerful weapon in the struggle for liberation. You are invited to use it.

Shelley Ettinger<br>February 1993

*Shelley Ettinger was a founding member of the Lesbian and Gay Labor Network. She is a managing editor of Workers World newspaper.*

\* For a full discussion of this struggle, see the pamphlet *Transgender Liberation: A Movement Whose Time Has Come*, by Leslie Feinberg. In it, Feinberg notes the enormous contribution this book made to the struggle for gender freedom.

# INTRODUCTION

Until a militant movement of lesbians and gay men arose to challenge it, there existed a generally accepted taboo in this country that homosexuality was not a fit topic for serious discussion.

The subject was long confined to psychiatric textbooks, whispered condemnations, degrading jokes, and veiled literary and historical references. The truth about homosexuality, and the roots and history of anti-gay prejudice, were hidden from gay and straight people alike.

The oppression of lesbians, gays and transgendered people began long ago. Since that time most gay people have been forced to hide their real selves behind a mask of heterosexual conformity. Thus lesbians and gays, deprived of their social and political identity like so many other oppressed groups, have been a largely invisible minority about whom the most prejudiced and distorted ideas flourished.

All this is changing, however, spurred by the historic Stonewall Rebellion in 1969 and the movement for lesbian and gay liberation that has exploded in the years since.

In late June of 1969, young transsexuals, transvestites, gay men and lesbians—Black, Latin and white—pushed to the wall by endless police raids on their social gathering places in New York City's Greenwich Village, fought back by the hundreds in four nights of street battles. This massive violent resistance to centuries-old oppression sent shock waves across the United States, Canada, Latin America, and Europe. Within months there were gay liberation groups in all the major population centers. Gay banners flew at all the many anti-war demonstrations of that period. For the first time open, proud gay people flocked to the defense of other oppressed people, demanding immediate freedom for Huey Newton, Angela Davis, and the many other political prisoners, gay and straight, languishing in the U.S.'s racist concentration-camp prison system.

Sexuality has, of course, always been a part of human experience. But attitudes toward it have differed tremendously in different times and places as a result of differing material circumstances. Homosexuality, in turn, has always been a part of sexuality, though not its most consistently predominant form. In most human societies in history it has been accepted. To understand how homosexuality came to be viewed as aberrant, it is important to examine the changing historical periods and their impact on sexual attitudes in general as well as on homosexuality in particular.

Thus, our approach here will be historical. We will attempt to focus on the changing attitudes toward sexuality and homosexuality as human society has evolved from its long pre-history—perhaps as long as 4 million years—into and through the last 4,000 to 8,000 years of much more rapid social change.

It will be necessary to confine our main attention to the societies of the so-called Western world. The reason for this is that available information concerning homosexuality in non-Western societies is sparse and often subject to disparate interpretations. It does seem clear, however, that nowhere else have attitudes toward homosexuality been as profoundly negative as they are in Western society.

Every phenomenon has a history. Development and transformation are characteristic of everything that exists. We believe that uncovering the history of lesbian and gay oppression will help bring that oppression to an end.

The facts clearly show that the persecution of homosexuals is not an immutable fact of all human history. Anti-gay prejudices have not always existed. They need not continue to exist in the future.

In modern times one of the first attempts to end lesbian and gay oppression was made by the leaders of the great socialist revolution in Russia. As we will see in Chapter 6, the Bolshevik leaders of the Soviet Union made a bold, serious attempt to end the persecution of homosexuals; this effort was unfortunately turned back by those who rose to power afterward.

In reading the historical analysis that follows, a number of points should be kept in mind. First, the terms "primitive" and "primitive communism" will be used to describe societies that exist at a very low level of technological development. All human societies were "primitive" in this sense for the first 3 million to 4 million years of humanity's existence. Even today a few small, isolated groups in various parts of the world continue to live at this low level of development.

The primitive level of technology possessed by these groups should not, however, blind us to the very humane character of their social relations. Primitive societies were communal. Food and other necessities of life were shared equally. There was no division between haves and have-nots. Under the prevailing conditions of scarcity there was general equality among men and women. Each member of the group, male and female alike, was needed to help produce the daily wherewithal for the continuance of life. In primitive societies the main struggle was against nature rather than human being against human being, as it became with the development of class society.

Second, almost all anthropological and historical reports exhibit a strong bias with regard to women and to homosexuality. Although women and men lived together as equals for most of the long period of human pre-history, the development of society into classes of rich and poor—a very recent development beginning 4,000 to 8,000 years ago—brought with it the subjugation of women. Since that time very prejudicial attitudes toward them have dominated society. Today even the most "objective" anthropological and historical works tend to ignore the contributions and achievements of women.

The same thing is true with regard to homosexuals and homosexuality. Anthropology and history are social sciences, subject to all the prejudices and biased viewpoints of the societies in which they exist. It is not unusual to come across the most negative and prejudiced references to homosexuality in historical and anthropological reports. Yet, even though biased in subject matter and method, these reports make it clear that homosexuality has always been a part of human sexuality; they suggest that primitive people viewed sexuality in a very different way than it is viewed today.

Third, as the word "homosexuality" is used in this book, it means the sexual and/or amorous attraction of people of the same sex. It may or may not include overt sexual acts and the people involved may or may not also be attracted to members of the opposite sex.

Sex researcher Alfred Kinsey and his associates, in addition to documenting the existence of homosexual behavior among many other animal species besides our own (especially those higher on the phylogenetic scale), studied 5,000 men and 6,000 women in an attempt to determine the extent of homosexual activity in the U.S. They found that while only about 4 percent of their male sample were exclusively homosexual throughout their lifetimes, 37 percent had had at least one homosexual experience to the point of orgasm. Another 13 percent who had never had an actual homosexual experience admitted to having had homosexual feelings to one extent or another. The percentages among the women were lower but still sizable. This suggested to Kinsey that a significant part of the population is bisexual rather than exclusively homosexual or heterosexual.

The work of Kinsey and other sex researchers helps to highlight the significance of lesbian and gay oppression as a major social problem. Whatever percentages are used, and contemporary evidence suggests that Kinsey's figures were far too low, the issue clearly affects, directly and indirectly, tens of millions of people in the United States alone.

It is generally assumed that "feminine" characteristics in men and "masculine" characteristics in women are symptomatic of homosexuality. This is far from a very meaningful generalization. Such a formulation obscures the fact that all men and women exhibit, to varying degrees, characteristics generally associated with the opposite sex. It is more accurate to say that among lesbian and gay people there are a greater proportion who do not fit the sexual stereotypes of how men and women are "supposed" to act and be. These stereotypes, or sex roles, are a product of class society, which has distorted the social positions of men and women as well as their relations with each other from the very start.

Beyond the physiological differences, factors related to maternity, and the sexual division of labor, class society has added artificial barriers between the sexes and distorted sexual values of all sorts. Men have come to be looked upon as strong, self-contained, independent and competent. Women are portrayed as weak, given to emotional excess, dependent and helpless. Of course most women and men do not fit such ridiculous caricatures of human beings. But lesbians and gay men, even more than heterosexuals, constitute a real challenge to these rigid, fallacious conceptions of masculinity and femininity.

# Homosexuality in Primitive Society

In order to get a real feeling for life in primitive society it is necessary to divest ourselves of a number of preconceptions that almost all of us hold on the basis of having grown up and lived in a capitalist society. For example, most people accept the existence of families, governments and privately owned property without a second thought. Yet these particular institutions and many others are fairly recent developments when measured against the several million years of human life on this planet. They have only come into existence in the past few thousand years and are closely related, as we shall see, to the development of class society.

The people of pre-class society, or what Marxists call the period of primitive communism, left us no written records of their lives and times. Writing was an invention that coincided with the rise of class society. Yet we have learned a great deal about what life must have been like during that long period by studying the reports of anthropologists, explorers and missionaries who, for centuries now, have been recording their impressions of life among isolated human groups—societies that have remained relatively untouched by the general advance of civilization.

Some of these tribal societies are only now giving way before the merciless pressures of class society in areas like the Outback of Australia, the dense jungles of the Philippines, various Arctic regions, and the interior regions of South America and Africa. Others, like the many tribal groupings of North America, have been decimated and, in some cases, totally annihilated by the frenzied forces of capitalist exploitation.

The observations that have been made of these widely scattered groups are sufficient to give us confidence in a few general characterizations, the most important of which were first advanced over 100 years ago by Frederick Engels in his great work *The Origin of the Family, Private Property, and the State.*

Engels noted that one of the most striking features of primitive societies was the profound respect and honor accorded women. The sexual division of labor that existed in primitive society was based on material conditions, mainly the fact that women were the childbearers and for this reason tended to stay nearer the home. But the home was not the socially isolated and restricting place it tends to be in capitalist society. Rather, it was the center of communal life and social activity.

It was primarily but not exclusively the men who hunted. The women's tasks were of a more cooperative and social nature and their contributions to the struggle for survival were enormous. There is strong evidence that women were the developers of language, the domesticators of animals, the cultivators of plants and the first builders of dwellings. In all probability, it was the innovations, inventions and discoveries of women that brought various primitive groups to the threshold of class society.

### The Basis of Matriarchal Social Order

All this, however, is not the primary reason Engels characterized primitive society as *matriarchal*. It is true that women were often among the leading members of these groups. And missionaries and anthropologists stepping out of the male-dominated world of capitalist society have on occasion been flabbergasted to see the men they mistook for tribal chiefs—who were often, in reality, only the leaders of hunting or war parties—consulting with councils of women on matters of importance.

But the matriarchy did not imply the rule of women over men. Tribal societies had no rulers, male or female—nothing like the parade of pharaohs, emperors, kings, czars and presidents that class society has generated. What authority the leading women and men had was based on their proven abilities and the voluntary respect thus accorded them. There were no armies or police organizations to carry out orders for them or protect them should the tribal rank and file turn against them. Neither did they live in regal splendor on the backs of those who worked. In Engels' words, "The shabbiest police servant in the civilized state has more 'authority' than all the organs of gentile [tribal] society put together; but the most powerful prince and the greatest statesman or general of civilization may well envy the humblest gentile chief for the uncoerced and undisputed respect that is paid to him."

What basically defined matriarchal society were the kinship relations. Paternity and the procreative function of sexual intercourse were not understood in primitive societies and sexual relationships seem not to have included cohabitation until very late in the period of primitive communism. Thus blood descent was only traceable through the mother. Tribal organization centered around mothers and their children. Care of children was a cooperative effort by all the women and their brothers. The children's fathers were, at most, visitors in the communal home of the mothers and the mothers' blood relations. The fathers lived with their own sisters and helped care for their sisters' children.

And this is a good place to remind ourselves that any impulse to make a moral judgment about this form of social organization would be foolish in the extreme. Though such an arrangement is an outrage from the standpoint of patriarchal monogamy (the father-dominated family of class society), it was perfectly acceptable to our tribal ancestors. It was a form of social organization that corresponded to their material conditions. In fact, they knew of no other way to live.

In such a social context, with the role of sexual intercourse in the production of children not understood, and with the marriage institution constituting little more than brief visits for purposes of mating, it would certainly be a reasonable assumption that homosexuality would have been an acceptable form of sexual expression. And indeed, this appears to have been the case.

## Manifestations of Homosexuality in Primitive Society

The existence of homosexuality among primitive peoples is, from the evidence, indisputable and in fact appears to have been widespread. Claude Levi-Strauss, a modern leader of the bourgeois school of anthropology, reports on the practice of homosexuality among the Nambikawara people of central Brazil in his book *Tristes Tropiques*. He writes, "These relations, common among the younger men, are carried out with a publicity uncommon in the case of more normal relations..." He further describes these homosexual affairs as "...childishness and of no serious account."

Levi-Strauss gives no indication in his writings of holding anything other than the standard anti-gay prejudices of his own culture and this necessarily brings into question his evaluation of what he has seen. But the observation itself certainly seems to support the view that homosexuality was an accepted and widespread form of sexual expression among primitive people. And although Levi-Strauss leaves it unsaid, it is well established that almost all primitive peoples treat their sexual activities, homosexual and heterosexual, with a casualness that is often disturbing to Christian missionaries and bourgeois anthropologists.

Bronislaw Malinowski, who is another important figure in the field of bourgeois anthropology, gives evidence of homosexuality among a number of Pacific Island peoples, but says that "unnatural conditions" give rise to it and that most of the native peoples view it with "contempt and repugnance." These assertions, however, must remain in question. Malinowski's discussions of homosexuality and sexuality in general reek of moral puritanism, a position very alien to the views of most primitive peoples. Further, the whole question of what constitutes "unnatural conditions" is certainly open to debate. To a resident of Manhattan, for example, the idea that there may be "unnatural conditions" on the South Sea Islands where Malinowski found homosexuality is open to question, to say the least.

In their book *Patterns of Sexual Behavior,* psychologists Ford and Beach surveyed reports on 76 primitive societies for attitudes toward homosexuality. The information was scant regarding lesbianism. Regarding male homosexuality they found that in roughly two-thirds of the 76 societies homosexual activity of one kind or another was considered to be normal and socially acceptable, at least for some members of the group. While such a finding may sound like an overestimation to some, it is in reality a conservative figure if you consider that it is based on the sort of biased reports to which we have already alluded.

In their discussion Ford and Beach mention one tribal society, probably not unique, where homosexual and heterosexual relationships coexist equally:

Among the Siwans of Africa ... all men and boys engage in anal intercourse. They adopt the feminine role only in strictly sexual situations and males are singled out as peculiar if they do not indulge in these homosexual activities. Prominent Siwan men lend their sons to each other, and they talk about their masculine love affairs as openly as they discuss their love of women. Both married and unmarried males are expected to have both homosexual and heterosexual affairs.

Many observers have noted that among many primitive peoples, such as the Papuans, the Keraki and the Kiwai of New Guinea, sexual acts between the younger and older men are an essential part of the rites of passage into adulthood.

Tobias Schneebaum's observations of a primitive group in South America are the only anthropological reports we know of by an openly gay man. Unprejudiced toward forms of sexual expression many of his fellow explorers find abhorrent and tend to ignore or minimize, Schneebaum was able to make contact with and live for a time among a homosexually oriented and previously totally isolated tribal group, the Amarakaeri people of eastern Peru. In his book *Keep the River on Your Right* and in a number of anthropological reports, Schneebaum describes this people's sexual customs. Amarakaeri women and children sleep apart from the men, as is common in many primitive tribal groups. Love-making in this tribe, however, is almost exclusively homosexual among both men and women. Only on ceremonial occasions two or three times a year are heterosexual acts performed.

## Transvestism—A Common Phenomenon Among Primitive Peoples

Many anthropologists who would probably be blind to less blatant manifestations have been confronted by a public, institutionalized form of homosexuality in tribe after tribe. Literally hundreds of anthropological reports on societies scattered over all the continents mention the *berdache* phenomenon. It is impossible to ignore the special status accorded these male and female transvestites by so many primitive people.

The German scholar Hermann Bauman has documented the existence of berdaches among most of the Indian nations of North

America. He says that they were highly respected and often played a ritual sex role with non-berdache men in religious ceremonies. He further documents the existence of male and female transvestites who acted as shamans or "witch doctors" among many African tribes.

In his book *The Origin and Development of the Moral Ideas* Edward Westermarck writes: "There is no indication that the North American aborigines attached any opprobrium to men who had intercourse with those members of their own sex who had assumed the dress and habits of women. In Kadiak such a companion was on the contrary regarded as a great acquisition; and the effeminate men, far from being despised, were held in repute by the people, most of them being wizards." He further notes, "The Sioux, Sacs, and Fox Indians give once a year or oftener, a feast to the Berdache. ..."

Further substantiating the widespread character of this phenomenon in aboriginal North America, the Jesuit missionary Lafitan reported in 1724: "If some women are found possessing virile courage, and glorying in the profession of war ... there exist also men so cowardly as to live like women. Among the Illinois, among the Sioux, in Louisiana, in Florida, and in Yucatan, there are found youths who adopt the garb of women ... and who think themselves honoured in stooping to all their occupations. ..." Lafitan's comments reflect a rather common combination of prejudices. People who have strong sexist attitudes are also usually virulently anti-gay and vice versa.

The prominent anthropologist James Frazer writes in his work *Adonis, Attis, and Osiris:* "effeminate sorcerers or priests ... are found among the Sea Dyaks of Borneo, the Bugis of South Celebes, the Patagonians of South America. ... In Madagascar we hear of effeminate men who wore female attire and acted as women, thinking thereby to do God service. In the kingdom of the Congo there was a sacrificial priest who commonly dressed as a woman."

Our main purpose in quoting the preceding material has been to demonstrate that homosexuality is not alien to humans living in the "natural" setting of primitive society. Those who hold to the position that homosexuality is "unnatural" or the result of unnatural conditions or that it is a mental illness are hard pressed to explain the widespread acceptance of homosexuality among primitive peoples.

One of the most widely held ideas about homosexuality is that it is an abnormality or a sickness, that it somehow violates the "natural order" of things. It has been argued that homosexuality becomes widespread when a society is in decline and thus homosexuality is somehow connected with decadence and social disintegration. However, not only was homosexuality acceptable among many primitive peoples but it is found in virtually every human grouping in every period that has been examined in any detail.

## Homosexuality Among Women in Primitive Society

A final word should be said about homosexuality among women in primitive societies. Although there is much less information available and although what there is contains less detail, the phenomenon is far from uncommon. The sexist Jesuit Lafitan, whose shock at the extent of male "effeminacy" among Indian tribes is clear from the excerpt of his writing quoted above, was equally outraged by the many Indian "Amazons" (women who fought and hunted with the men) he observed. Many other investigators have included such brief observations as well as examples of homosexuality among tribal women who did not assume male dress or behavior.

In an article on Samoan women, Margaret Mead observes that "casual homosexual relations between girls never assumed any long-time importance. On the part of growing girls or women who were working together they were regarded as a pleasant and natural diversion, just tinged with the salacious." Mead indicates that heterosexual relations in Samoa were equally casual, complicated only "by children and the place of marriage in the economic and social structure of the village."

Engels postulated that at the dawn of human society, and for some length of time into the period of primitive communism, human sexual behavior was characterized by "promiscuous intercourse" and a bit later by "group marriage":

> And indeed, what do we find as the oldest, most primitive form of the family, of which undeniable evidence can be found in history, and which even today can be studied here and there? Group marriage, the form in which whole groups of men and whole groups of women belong to one another, and which leaves

but little scope for jealousy. ... However, the forms of group marriage known to us are accompanied by such peculiarly complicated conditions that they necessarily point to simpler forms of sexual relations and thus, in the last analysis, to a period of promiscuous intercourse corresponding to the period of transition from animality to humanity.

The sexual "casualness" that Margaret Mead speaks of among the Samoans, on which many other observers of primitive society have also commented, seems clearly to have been a general characteristic of pre-class sexuality. Engels suggests that jealousy and possessiveness have their root in the institution of private property. However, what little of the necessities of life there was under under primitive communism, was held in common. Sharing was an unquestioned and necessary way of life. Modern humanity, having witnessed all too vividly the suffering and destruction wrought by those contemporary giants of private property who seek ownership of the whole world, will one day in the not too distant future begin the reinstitution of communism—this time based on material plenty rather than the scarcity of prehistoric times.

# The Overthrow of the Matriarchy and Early Class Society

In the preceding chapter we acquainted ourselves with some of the general features of primitive society. For primitive peoples, the struggle against nature, the struggle to survive, was more or less a full-time job for everyone. The development of technology to the level where more material wealth could be produced than was immediately needed for the survival of the tribe brought a fundamental change to human relations.

It was on the basis of this surplus accumulation of material wealth in the form of herds of domesticated animals, storage sheds of grain and other useful products that classes arose. The surplus wealth, now more and more in the possession of individuals, became a source of power for a minority. With the gradual development of private property, over a very long historical period actually, relations of exploitation were formed between the haves and the have-nots. The new property relations were, however, insupportable and unworkable without consequent changes in kinship relations, sexual relations, and religious attitudes and practices.

This world historic process had as its material precondition in any particular society the accumulation of surplus among the leading male members of the tribe. At a certain point it became clear that husbandry and farming yielded greater material gains than hunting. The women, who had developed the techniques of animal domestication and breeding and agriculture to a high level, were then gradually supplanted by the men. This was not because the men consciously planned it that way. Nor does it indicate any kind of sexual struggle between men and women for dominance. This was not the case. It was material conditions, primarily the facts that men had more experience with larger animals and thus had charge of the cattle while the women tended the smaller (and less valuable) barnyard animals and that the men, being warriors, were in a better position to institute the practice of using captured foes as slaves. These factors and others were the material basis of the enrichment of male tribal leaders over and against the women and the tribe as a whole.

The crux of the struggle against the matriarchal organization of society was over the question of the lineage of children. Even in the later stages of matriarchal society, when a family organization more like what we know today had evolved, descent continued to be through the mother. So the husband's wealth went not to his own children but to the children of his sister. At a certain point the development of purchase marriage added further pressures on the existing system of determining descent. The men not only wanted their wealth to go to their own children but, as the custom of purchasing brides with cattle evolved, they wanted a guarantee of possession of the children even if the marriage should end. This guarantee could only be effected by the establishment of patrilineal descent.

## Private Property and the Degradation of Sexuality

So the development of private property not only brought forth economic inequalities that set the stage for class society but also had the effect of replacing the matriarchal order with one dominated by men. And further changes followed.

Sexual relations in matriarchal society, though subject to some restrictions, were much less restricted and less laden with strong emotional overtones than they have become in class society. For example, women, equally with men, had the right to choose new partners if their interest in the old ones waned. And most important, under the matriarchy this right was not abridged by economic dependency on the husband.

Sexual expression could be casual as long as sexual practices did not conflict with the property interests of the tribal leaders. But casual, relaxed attitudes toward the expression of heterosexuality did contradict the interests of the new propertied chiefs. So seriously did the chiefs take the question of passing on their wealth and name that the demand for wifely monogamy assumed a primary importance among them. Only thus could the paternity of the children be determined with complete certainty. Homosexual relations also posed the question of inheritance of property outside of the ordered tribal lineage.

Emotions and sexual feelings for the first time in history came under harsh social-class scrutiny and stringent sexual prohititions were erected. Shame, guilt and fear began to be connected with sex. What had been casual, spontaneous and natural in the true sense of the word became the source of conflict, and ultimately, persecution, when forced into the confines of patriarchal class society. With the rise of private property the natural became "unnatural."

Sexual jealousy, that powerful, destructive, and largely irrational feeling that haunts the love relationships of class society, was implicit in the new attitude of the husband toward his wife and children. They, like his cattle and his stores of grain, had become his private property. In fact, in some early legal codes rape was considered a crime of theft.

Sexuality in general assumed a negative social significance it had never before had. It was a form of personal expression that was incompatible with the new patriarchal order except within the rigidly prescribed limits of the male-dominated monogamous family. And this fact, it seems likely, is what made homosexuality a social and political issue in class society in a way it had never been before.

Now it is true that heterosexuality has been the more prevalent form of sexual expression in most societies. And it is also true that homosexuality does not preclude heterosexual behavior for purposes of procreation (as we saw with the Amarakaeri tribe of South America) or as a coexisting form of sexual expression (as with the Siwan people of Africa). Yet homosexual activity does presuppose a certain degree of freedom, if only the freedom to search out partners. And this freedom was now decisively curtailed for women by the imposition of monogamy on them.

Sexual restrictions on men have, of course, never been as severe as those on women. But, having just won the right to bequeath his name and wealth to his son—to have his name and his honor live after him—the father could not have been pleased at the prospect of a homosexual son who might never produce heirs of his own.

In fact, there is little doubt that it was just such a fear that constituted the basis of the development of a prohibition against male homosexuality.

Of course, the change did not occur all at once. The new attitudes evolved very slowly, in fact. Their development roughly paralleled certain changes in ancient religious belief and practice.

## The Role of Religion in Primitive Society

Primitive people were relatively ignorant of the operation of natural laws. The onslaught of natural forces was a constant threat before which they were relatively helpless. Under such conditions religious ideas and practices played a far more important role than they do today. Primitive people believed in magic, in spirits, and evolved elaborate rituals which were naive and largely irrational attempts to gain some control over natural and social forces. Their objects of worship included various animals, ancestors, demons, mythic superhumans, sky gods and goddesses, and even things like rocks, trees and grottos. A prominent ceremony for many tribes was the fertility rite in which women and female deities were accorded special honors for their ability to bring forth new life.

In addition, many observers have noted the connection between sexuality and religious feeling among primitive peoples. Ritual heterosexual and homosexual practices were often part of primitive religious worship. Transvestites of both sexes often played important roles in these ceremonies. According to Edward Westermarck, who wrote about homosexuality at the turn of this century: "Among the Illinois Indians, the effeminate men assist in all the juggleries and the solemn dance in honor of the calumet, or sacred tobacco pipe, for which the Indians have such a deference. ... They are called into the councils of the Indians, and nothing can be decided without their advice: for because of their extraordinary manner of living they are looked upon as *manitous,* or supernatural beings, and persons of consequence."

Other investigators have made similar observations about the role of berdaches. According to a military doctor who was stationed among the Pueblo Indians of Mexico in 1850, *mujerados* or "feminized men" were "indispensable for the religious orgies which were celebrated among the Pueblo Indians. ... These Saturnalia take place in the spring of every year and are kept with the greatest secrecy from the observation of non-Indians." He further reported: "To be a mujerado is no disgrace to a Pueblo Indian. On the contrary, he enjoys the protection of his tribes-people, and is accorded a certain amount of honor."

Observations of similar attitudes and practices have been reported about such diverse societies as the Patagonians of South America, the ancient Scandinavians, and the Konyaga Eskimos. Although references to the religious activity of primitive women are scarce, there are reports that suggest that transvestite women were also regarded as having special religious powers. One report in a turn of the century work on homosexuality by Edward Carpenter says that such women existed in North African communities and elsewhere.

As classes of rich and poor evolved all of society was affected. The transformation was a protracted one, actually extending over thousands of years from the first beginnings of animal domestication and plant cultivation to the final consolidation of class divisions with the establishment of organizations of repression—states—that had the specific purpose of defending and enforcing the new slave-based social order.

## The Transformation of Ancient Religion

Religion, too, underwent a transformation. The ancient religious practices and beliefs very gradually changed under the influence of changing social conditions, until they more adequately reflected the new social order. Just as it had taken over the surplus material wealth of society, the new dominant class gradually gained influence over religious life. In some cases members of the slave-owning class became priests themselves and set up religious organizations under their own control. In other cases their control was indirect. These new religious organizations had political and economic functions and sometimes even exercised state political power in places where their numbers included powerful slave owners or commercial interests.

Like any new social phenomenon, the religious organizations of early class society retained something of the old. Even where the temple had become, in reality, a political tool for repression against the masses of poor people, many of the old religious rites, including various sexual rites, continued.

There was, however, an important new element even in the sexual rites. In many of the ancient city-states of Mesopotamia and elsewhere, temples of worship were organized where, for a price, the faithful could have sexual intercourse with the gods and goddesses. Now it is important here to remind the reader that this ritual sexuality was very definitely considered primarily a religious act by those who engaged in it. The strong link between religious feelings and ritual sexuality had truly ancient origins in the ritual sexuality of primitive society. The priests and priestesses who engaged in these rites were believed to be possessed or taken over by a god or goddess. The sexual act was understood to be an act of communion between the worshipper and the divinity.

The exchange of money in these ceremonies was the new and significant element. It reflected the development of class relations and it limited the participation of the masses of poor, among whom the older and less expensive forms of sexually oriented religious worship continued. It also led to the characterization of these priests and priestesses by later investigators as "temple prostitutes." The introduction of sexual intercourse for money had profound significance as a historic turning point and a background for understanding present-day sexual attitudes. This new commercial transaction really did mean that sex was no longer free. And though the masses of poor people continued on in the old ways, in the long run this new custom of the ruling classes forced its influence down among the masses. Together with other new factors, such as the demand of monogamy and hostility toward homosexuality, it produced great distortions in sexual relations among the people.

But the so-called temple prostitutes, those women and men who performed homosexual and heterosexual acts in the temples for money, were completely unlike the prostitutes of contemporary society. In terms of their social position they had much more in common with the berdaches and shamans of primitive society. They were honored and esteemed and well cared for. Their lives were free of the degradation and oppression that in later times became the lot of those forced by poverty to sell their bodies for money.

The practice of sexual worship was common in the ancient societies of Egypt, Babylonia, Assyria, Canaan, Chaldea, Sumeria, Greece and elsewhere. The myths surrounding various gods and goddesses of these nations often contained material of a sexual nature. The myths were, of course, a creation and reflection of human society. This is very evident in a piece of historical evidence on homosexuality described by Hans Licht in his book *Sexual Life in Ancient Greece:*

> The oldest literary testimony hitherto known dates back more than 4,500 years, and is to be found in an Egyptian papyrus which proves not only that paederasty [i.e., male homosexuality] was at that time widespread in Egypt but also that it was presumed to exist amongst the gods as a matter of course.

By the time Egypt and these other ancient lands had become centers of trade and culture, the leading figures in all areas of their social and political life were, with few exceptions, men. The nation of Egypt retained more vestiges of the matriarchy for a longer time than other nations, but it was also among the first of these slave societies to arise. By and large, the world historic overthrow of the matriarchy was victorious. The social position of women was reduced to that of child-bearers and domestic servants.

# The Evolution of Patriarchal Religion

Among the earliest transformations from primitive society was the system of slave labor in the early class societies of the eastern Mediterranean and the so-called Fertile Crescent area of the Middle East. The slaves, gathered together on farms and in mining areas by the hundreds and thousands, were treated like beasts of burden and so did not by and large work energetically or well. What brought about their widespread use in agriculture, mining and primitive commodity production was the relatively low price at which they could be purchased and maintained. Capture of foreign peoples was the main source of this cheap supply of labor. So the slave-based economic system was a powerful stimulus to warfare between neighboring city-states. In fact, wars of conquest and pillage raged almost continuously among the ancient nations of Mesopotamia, Greece and elsewhere.

The Hebrews were originally one of many Semitic tribes that migrated out of Arabia into the Fertile Crescent region about 1000 B.C. This particular tribe gradually conquered and settled in the land of Canaan, a part of Palestine. At this point the originally nomadic people put down roots and began its evolution into a nation of peasants and traders. Situated as the new nation was astride the trade routes connecting Syria, Egypt, Babylonia and other nations, commerce quickly became a source of great wealth. Yet there was also a negative side to this valuable piece of geography which was to prove disastrous.

The powerful ancient nations of this area were often at war with each other, and the Palestinian plain that lay between them was the site of many of their clashes. The Hebrew nation could not long remain unweakened by the continual invasions of its territory, the drain on its wealth for military expenditures, and the carrying off of its peasantry to become slaves in the lands of the invaders. Finally, with the victory of the Babylonians over the Hebrew stronghold of Jerusalem, the nation was completely dismantled. Much of the population of the city was forced to move to Babylon—the so-called Babylonian exile.

Until this historic point, there was no religion among the Mideastern peoples that truly reflected the patriarchal character of these societies. Certainly the religion of the Hebrews was in no fundamental way distinguishable from the other tribal-based religions of that area and time. They had their special tribal deity (Yahweh) but also worshipped other deities and practiced ritual sexuality, both heterosexual and homosexual.

It was suggested in the last chapter that the first steps toward a fundamental change in religious practices had been taken with the assumption of control of religious institutions by the slave-owning classes of the Mideastern nations and with the introduction of monetary considerations into religious worship (for example, "temple prostitution" and "priestly" commercial activity). Still, however, the old matriarchal receptivity toward religion-connected sexual expression continued to prevail and among the deities there continued to be many powerful goddesses, hermaphroditic figures, and homosexually inclined divinities of both sexes.

## Patriarchal Monotheism—An Idea Whose Time Had Come

Karl Kautsky suggests in his important work *The Foundations of Christianity* that the concept of patriarchal monotheism—the idea of a single male god—was developing elsewhere with less intensity at the time it was fervently embraced by the post-exilic Hebrews. He cites the brief appearance of monotheism in Egypt during the reign of Akenaton and the secret occult doctrines of the Babylonian priests. But, he notes, unlike the priestly castes of Babylonia and Egypt who had a material interest in preserving the polytheistic doctrines on which their power and privilege rested, the post-exilic Jewish religious leaders were open to new ideas. They had nothing to lose.

The end of the Babylonian exile came when Babylon itself was conquered by the Persians under King Cyrus. The exiled Jews were permitted to return to Jerusalem and re-establish their trading enterprises. Kautsky comments: "...religion now necessarily became the more prominent among the Jews by reason of the fact that the destruction of their national independence left only their common national worship as the sole bond still uniting the nation. The priesthood of this worship now constituted the only central organization retaining any authority in the eyes of the entire people." The concept that now emerged of one god—a wrathful male deity—was not totally new. It bore some resemblance to the earlier tribal deity Yahweh. Much of the mythology surrounding it was borrowed from Babylonian religious myths.

Yet the assertion made on behalf of this god, that he was master of the universe and of all peoples and was the one and only true god, was new. It reflected the need of a beleaguered nation to weld together a spiritual force strong enough to ensure national survival. It also reflected—almost like a mirror—the essence of political relations in slave society. The king, pharaoh, or emperor was the all-powerful father. To him went all tribute and honor. Woe to the pitiful subject who defied "His" will.

The creation of "the one true God" brought with it the destruction of all the vestiges of matriarchal religious practices. Wainwright Churchill points out in his book *Homosexual Behavior Among Males* that of the 36 crimes punishable by death in the post-exilic Jewish Mosaic Law, fully half concerned sexual acts of one kind or another. The punishment for homosexual acts was death by stoning, considered the most severe possible punishment for any crime. Churchill suggests that this radical moral transformation was, at least in part, based on the need of the Jews to distinguish themselves in a decisive way from the surrounding hostile nations that threatened to overwhelm them culturally as well as militarily. He notes, "In Talmudic writings homosexuality is associated with 'the way of the Canaanite,' the way of the Chaldean—the way of the 'heathen'." Yet the homosexual taboo bears a more general significance too. The special conditions of the development of the Jewish nation made it possible for patriarchal monotheism to take hold here first. Within a relatively short historical period, however, monotheism and prohibitions against sexuality and especially homosexuality would come to dominate all of Western class society.

## Sexuality and Homosexuality in Classical Greece

In the same general period that the Hebrews were transforming their religious beliefs so radically, the Greek city-states were developing in a very different way. As with virtually every ancient people, the early tribal peoples of Greece were organized on a matriarchal basis and homosexuality is known to have existed among them. Here, too, ritual sexuality was a part of religious practices. As slave society developed there was a tendency for these rites to evolve into "temple prostitution" although many cultic sexual rites that did not involve the exchange of money continued among the people.

Actually, religion in the Greek city-states never became the powerful institution it was in the great commercial centers of the Middle East. By the time the various Greek city-states began growing wealthy on the basis of plunder, slave labor and trade, the temple priesthoods were hemmed in on the one side by scores of popular cultic religions, some dating from matriarchal times, and on the other by schools of secular philosophers who played an important role in politics, education and the social life of the time.

With patriarchal "moral authority" so decentralized in Greece, it is not to be wondered at that important remnants of tribal culture remained and coexisted with the newer forms for an extended period. Because the priests were weak, sexuality was not so profoundly politicized as it was elsewhere. For example, the Greeks continued to take delight in the naked human body far into patriarchal times. Elsewhere nudity had become shameful.

Whereas our problem with most of the ancient civilizations is that so little has been recorded about their sexual customs, we know a great deal about Hellenic Greece. We know, for example, that not only was homosexuality widespread in many of the Greek city-states but also that there were whole armies composed of pairs of homosexual lovers. Such, for example, was the Sacred Band of Thebes, which fought victoriously for over 30 years until the whole army was annihilated in 338 B.C. by King Phillip's much larger Macedonian army.

Plutarch reported that lesbian relationships among the women of Sparta were common. Also, many examples of classical Greek literature, painting and pottery have survived from as early as the

5th century B.C. They give clear testimony to the existence of lesbian love in many of the Greek communities of that period. In the religious and historical mythology of Greece there are many examples of homosexual relationships among gods and men. Among the people of various Greek cities a number of mythic homosexual and hermaphroditic figures were honored with yearly festivals. For example, Hyacinthus, a youth loved by the god Apollo according to Greek mythology, was honored each year in Sparta.

Two Greek city-states bear special mention with regard to the historical development of sexually repressive attitudes. Both Sparta and Athens made use of slave labor. In Athens, however, the system was much more highly developed. In Sparta women still retained a high measure of social equality. Both girls and boys in Sparta received athletic and military training. Both women and men had great sexual freedom. According to Engels both sexes had the right to have more than one sexual partner. He points out that this was clearly a holdover from the primitive practice of group marriage. We also know that homosexual relations among both women and men were common.

There existed an institutionalized form of sexual relationship between youths and men in Sparta that in all probability harked back to tribal puberty rites. The older of the two was morally responsible for the younger's conduct and development. The older was supposed to aid in the younger's education and to provide a model for him to aspire to. If the youth's parents were absent, the youth could be represented by his lover in the public assembly. In battle the two were supposed to fight near each other. The youth's shortcomings in warfare or other pursuits were considered the responsibility of the lover, who could be punished for them.

## Slave Society—The Degradation of Women and Homosexuals

By way of contrast, in Athens the male-dominated monogamous family already prevailed. Engels describes it in these words: "...its final victory [is] one of the signs of the beginning of civilization. It is based on the supremacy of the man; its express aim is the begetting of children of undisputed paternity, this paternity being required in order that these children may in due time inherit their father's wealth as his natural heirs." This development in Athens brought the extreme subjugation of women. The contrast with Sparta is striking. The women of Athens had no sexual freedom. They were deprived of educational opportunities except for learning practical domestic skills and were generally confined to the back rooms or upper floors of their homes. Engels emphasizes that monogamy in class society has always meant, in practice, monogamy for the wife, overt or covert polygamy for the husband.

In addition, the expression of sexual feelings, even among men, began to be restricted in political ways. For example, male and female prostitutes whose motive was strictly monetary made their appearance on the streets of Athens. This development completed the transformation of sex into a readily saleable commodity, which began with the evolution of temple prostitution.

Another restriction that took legal form in the code of Solon was the prohibition against homosexual relations between free men and slaves. It is important to remember that the so-called "Athenian democracy" rested, in reality, on a mass of slaves about four times the size of the free citizenry. Thus this prohibition had the effect of severely curtailing the number of potential partners for homosexual intercourse. It also, of course, helped to sharpen the division between the classes and was actually a class prohibition more than a sexual one.

By Plato's time, many voices, including Plato's own in his later years, began to be raised against sexual freedom and against homosexuality. The society that was later to gain a wide reputation for its "abandonment" to "Greek love" had begun to reflect the full force of the sexual restrictions of patriarchal society.

# THE RISE OF CHRISTIANITY AND MEDIEVAL EUROPE

Early Rome, better than any of the other ancient city-states, learned how to turn war into the most profitable of business ventures. The great Roman Empire took shape on the basis of imperial conquest, encompassing at its height all the countries bordering the Mediterranean Sea and much of western Europe. Karl Kautsky summarizes the political character of this vast entity:

> There were very few places left in the Roman Empire that retained any remnants of political life after Caesar's victories, and these remnants also were soon wiped out by Caesar's successors. A vigorous political life was kept alive longest of all in Jerusalem, the largest city of Palestine. The most serious exertions were required to overthrow this last stronghold. ... After a long and stubborn siege the city of Jerusalem was razed to the ground in the year 70 A.D. ...

For some time before the destruction of Jerusalem, Rome had ceased expanding its borders. The Roman armies had their hands full trying to protect the already conquered lands from incursions by outside forces. The Roman ruling class was also faced with the problem of financing its armies, which were assuming more and more of a mercenary character, and trying to revitalize its agricultural system, which had more or less collapsed after free peasants were replaced by slave labor.

Kautsky adds:

> The entire policy of this tremendous empire was concentrated in the city of Rome alone. But who were the persons who had become the bearers of political life in that city? They were financiers who thought only of accumulating interest upon interest; aristocrats who staggered from one enjoyment to another enjoyment, who scorned all regular labor, all exertion, even the exer-

tion of governing or waging war; and finally, the Lumpenproletariat, who lived by selling their political power to the highest bidder.

Rome has been characterized by historians of the capitalist world as sexually decadent. It has even been argued that this was the cause of its downfall. It is true, of course, that the ruling class of Rome engaged in disgusting and sometimes murderous excesses in their continual search for new sensations. Yet the material basis of the slow disintegration was not "moral" decadence but the decadence of an economic and political system that became increasingly parasitic and untenable.

When the tiny Christian sects first appeared in Rome their base was almost entirely among the poor. Early Christianity, in fact, contained strong elements of collectivism and hatred of the rich. In addition, the Christians were, from the start, hostile to so-called "earthly temptations." One of their principal early proselytizers, Paul of Tarsus, hoped that "converts to Christ" would renounce sexuality totally, as he had done: "I say therefore to the unmarried and widows, it is good for them if they abide even as I. But if they cannot contain, let them marry: for it is better than to burn." If Paul wasn't exactly enthusiastic about heterosexual relations, his views on other forms of sexual expression were little short of hysterical. He wrote in his Epistle to the Romans, "God gave them up unto vile passions: for their women changed the natural use into that which is against nature: and likewise also the men, leaving the natural use of the woman, burned in their lust one toward another, men with men working unseemliness. ..."

Paul and the other early Christian leaders set a tone of extreme self-denial for themselves and their followers, supposedly in the interests of avoiding "sin" and assuring themselves a place in heaven. This aspect of the new religion had a particular appeal for certain members of the upper classes who had tasted all the exotic pleasures of Roman ruling-class life and had found them wanting, or had finally recoiled from them in belated disgust. More and more of these people became converts. The new religion, which developed a hierarchy of its own as it grew, adapted itself to its powerful and often financially generous new friends. Kautsky analyzes in detail in *The Foundations of Christianity* how this patriarchal creation was transformed over a period of several hundred years from a revolutionary movement of the poor into a state religion that served the rich.

## Homosexuality Becomes a State Crime

Emperor Alexander Severus, who ruled Rome at the beginning of the 3rd century A.D., was the first head of state to take a public stand against homosexuality. Though he was officially a pagan, his mother was a convert to Christianity and he was undoubtedly influenced by the anti-homosexual stance of the Christian Church. Early in his reign he ordered the mass arrest of male prostitutes and ordered the deportation of many homosexual men active in public life.

In 342 Emperor Constantine raised Christianity to the status of state religion. With this move he added to the arsenal of the Roman state apparatus a new and deadly instrument of repression. Religion in general has always been based on ignorance. To this, partriarchal religion added the factor of class oppression. With the elevation of Christianity to the direct service of state power the religious enslavement of the masses of poor and oppressed was guaranteed. The U.S. bourgeoisie's slogan "In God we trust" really means, "In religion we trust to keep the masses from rebelling."

Innumerable examples of Church doctrine and practice demonstrate this oppressing function clearly. Ecclesiastical demands for self-sacrifice, subservience to authority, mysticism and the promise of a heavenly afterlife in return for obedience help guarantee the maintenance of class rule without need for the continual threat of violence. Concerning women, patriarchal religions have advanced the most reactionary positions imaginable. The Catholic Church's wild opposition to equality for women has continued right to the present day.

The very next emperor after Constantine decreed the death penalty for homosexuality. In 390 Emperor Valentian instituted death by burning, a previously unknown mode of execution, for the "crime" of "sodomy." In 538 Emperor Justinian codified Roman law. In a climate of pessimism and fear provoked by the utter disintegration of Roman society and the collapse of the Empire, he prescribed torture, mutilation, and castration for homosexuals, as a prelude to execution. The edict stated, in part: "...since certain men, seized by diabolical incitement, practice among themselves the most disgraceful lusts, and act contrary to nature: we enjoin them ... to abstain ... so that they may not be visited by the just wrath of God ... with the result that cities perish with all their inhabitants. For because of such crimes there are famines, earthquakes, and pestilences." The bourgeois historian Edward Gibbon, who was surely no friend of gay people, had to admit in his *History of the Decline and Fall of the Roman Empire* that "the cruelty of [Justinian's] persecutions can scarcely be excused by the purity of his motives. ... A painful death was inflicted by the amputation of the sinful instrument, or the insertion of sharp reeds into the pores of most exquisite sensibility. ... A sentence of death and infamy was often founded on the slight and suspicious evidence of a child or a servant, and pederasty became the crime of those to whom no crime could be imputed."

Death by burning became a common punishment for "the sin so horrible it must not be mentioned in the presence of Christians." Contemporary gay researchers have begun uncovering evidence from the feudal period in Europe that the Church used the bugaboo of sexual perversion to justify many thousands of executions.

## The Tyranny of the Church in Feudal Europe

As the Roman slave-based system of production disintegrated it was gradually replaced by a more dynamic system. The feudal serf's labor was more productive than the slave's. In the first place, the serf had the right to own things, for example, household goods and tools. Equally important, a certain portion of the time the serfs worked for themselves. This was a great stimulus toward increasing production both by working harder and by improving productive techniques. The only incentive under the slave system had been a negative one: the lash.

The feudal system was at first composed largely of fiefs controlled by petty nobles to whom the serfs were tied. Trade between the various fiefdoms was not extensive. Therefore towns were few and of secondary importance.

But there was one powerful institution uniting most of feudal Europe. This is how Engels describes it in *Socialism: Utopian and*

*Scientific:* "The great international center of feudalism was the Roman Catholic Church. It united the whole of feudalized Western Europe, in spite of all internal wars, into one grand political system. ... It surrounded feudal institutions with the halo of divine consecration. It had organized its own hierarchy on the feudal model, and lastly, it was itself by far the most powerful feudal lord, holding, as it did, fully one-third of the soil of the Catholic world."

It is of interest in this regard that the Church's demand for celibacy of its priests and nuns had more to do with financial than moral considerations. The Church sought to ensure that it would be the only legitimate heir for whatever wealth its ordained members might possess.

Powerful though it was, the Church was far from universally accepted. There was occasional resistance to papal authority among both feudal lords and the peasant serfs. The lesser lords, especially, could not always keep possession of their own wealth against the greater greed of the Church fathers. A favored tactic of the Church during the period of the so-called Holy Inquisition, which began in 1233, was to accuse a rich nobleman whose lands and wealth it coveted of religious heresy or homosexuality—or both. The two charges were often made together and came to imply each other. The individual might or might not be "guilty"—that was usually beside the point. In the meantime, on the basis of the accusation alone, the Church permitted itself to seize the accused's property. In this way, what we today call gay-baiting became a powerful economic weapon in the hands of the Catholic Church.

This vicious tactic was connected to a very real problem the Church faced with regard to individual heretics, heretical movements and pagan religious cults that continued to exist mainly among the peasantry. These manifestations of opposition to the religious and political tyranny of the Church had class roots. They were nurtured by a peasantry which, oppressed as it was by the feudal system, did not quickly or willingly give up its joyous, pro-sexual religious rites for the gloomy puritanism of Catholic Rome.

In certain places at certain times the Church showed amazing flexibility in winning the peasants over. Gay liberationist Arthur Evans, in one of a series of articles on the feudal period, reports on the attempts of a local Catholic priest in Scotland to integrate the celebration of Jesus's resurrection with an earlier, pre-Christian celebration. The priest was arraigned before his bishop in 1282, according to Evans, "for conducting a ritual dance around a phallus at Easter time. The priest readily admitted the charge, and said it was the accustomed practice of the place. The priest was admonished, but not denied his position."

Thorkil Vanggaard presents graphic evidence of similar flexibility regarding pagan religious eroticism at a 12th century Christian Church in Denmark in his book *Phallos*. Vanggaard remarks that the survival of a large and very realistic stone phallus, which records show originally stood at the front door of the church (it now stands behind the apse), is almost miraculous. And Raymond de Becker has a photograph in his book *The Other Face of Love* of two men in an explicit sexual embrace. The photo is of a relief between two arches or window settings, part of the stone work of the Cathedral of St. Peter at Poitiers, France.

## Religious Prohibitions on Sexual Expression Took a Murderous Turn Under Feudalism

At first the anti-homosexual position of the Church was manifested mainly in warnings, such as this one addressed to a group of nuns in 423 by St. Augustine: "The love which you bear to one another ought not to be carnal." Soon, however, the clerical prohibitions acquired a more serious character. By 693 the Church in Spain was reaffirming Justinian's punishment for male homosexuals: castration followed by execution. New penalties for homosexuality among nuns were also being devised although they were not as severe as the penalties for male clerics.

By the 11th century, if not earlier, the Church had begun supplementing its "flexible" approach among the pagans with increasing repression. Arthur Evans describes two early "witch" trials, one in 1022 and the other in 1114, for which detailed written records exist. In the earlier trial, held at Orleans, the defendants were charged with holding "religious orgies." In the other trial, held at Bucy-le-long, the charge was conducting "homosexual rites." Evans and other investigators have described the existence of groups that continued to practice old, matriarchal religious rites in many parts of feudal Europe. Often an "Earth

Mother" goddess or other such female deity was the central figure of worship. If there were male deities, they were usually explicitly phallic. There is also evidence of ritual transvestism among some of these groups. These movements tended to reject the prevailing values that called for the subjugation of women and the persecution of homosexuality. In fact, there is a good deal of evidence that the ritual sexuality of their religious rites included homosexual practices. Some of these groups were openly hostile to the Church and state, challenging the need for a clergy, a government, marriage or an organized religious hierarchy.

Among these groups were the Luciferians in Austria, the Adamites in Bohemia, the Brethren of the Free Spirit in Germany, the Massalians in the Balkan area and the Bogomils in Bulgaria. Such groups also existed in Italy, the Netherlands, France, England and on the Iberian peninsula. One of these movements, the Cathars, became so widespread in southern France, where they were called Albigensians, that they attracted significant numbers of the feudal ruling class of that region. Such a challenge to the authority of the Catholic Church did not long remain unanswered.

In 1208 Pope Innocent III ordered the French king to wipe them out. Apparently not much encouragement was needed. Here is one historian's description of what happened: "The faithful were enjoying themselves depopulating the south of France, confiscating property, settling political quarrels, extending baronial domains, and always fighting under the banner of the one true God. The immediate supply of heretics lasted the crusaders twenty years and it is estimated that a million of them were exterminated before the end of the century."

While this was probably the largest campaign, similar murderous attacks were launched against most of the other groups, especially with the advent of the Holy Inquisition. The strong influence of the Church's anti-homosexual position on secular authority is shown in the following excerpts from French legal codes of the late 13th century: "If anyone is suspected of *bougrerie* [i.e., "sodomy"] the magistrate must seize him and send him to the bishop: and if he is convicted, he must be burnt, and all his goods confiscated to the baron...." With regard to lesbianism: "The woman who does this shall undergo mutilation for the first and second offences, and on her third conviction must be burnt. And all the goods of such offenders shall be the king's."

Although not a typical witch hunt, the persecution of Joan of Arc (1412-1431) is very significant from the point of view of the history of homosexual oppression. She was, in fact, charged with witchcraft and transvestism in addition to other political crimes. It was only when she resumed her rebellious mode of dress, after having given promises to reform, that she was executed by the authorities.

The so-called "witch trials" continued long after the Inquisition itself was over. They were taken up enthusiastically, in fact, by some of the Protestant Reformation movements that accompanied and facilitated the rise of capitalism. All manner of nightmarish tortures were devised to get the victims to "confess" and many, many people were tortured, maimed, and murdered. Evans says that estimates of the number killed range from several hundred thousand to several million. These practices finally more or less died out at the end of the 18th century.

## The Catholic Church was a Force of Feudal Repression

So it can be seen that the Medieval Church, in conjunction with the feudal ruling class as a whole, raised the persecution of homosexuals to a hysterical pitch that has set the tone for Western attitudes and practice ever since. A number of contemporary anti-gay words such as faggot, fairy, punk and bugger originated during this period. As we have noted, the anti-homosexual frenzy manifested by the Medieval Church was based, at least in part, on the persistence of old matriarchal religious practices well into the epoch of patriarchy. Such manifestations of the Old Religion were probably especially attractive to oppressed women and to gay men. They constituted a threat to patriarchal Catholicism and the general social order that rested on the submission of the peasant serfs to the authority of the feudal barons and on the subjugation of women. Women who refused to be submissive, and men and women who violated the sexual roles expected of them, were persecuted for it.

It should be noted that not all those thousands who were charged, convicted and executed for homosexual practices were in fact guilty of them. Without a doubt, the Church and state used the accusations against both homosexual and heterosexual enemies, people whose lands were coveted or against whom there were personal grudges. They were also able to use gay men and lesbians as scapegoats for the problems of society just as ruling classes throughout history have done with other groups of oppressed people.

In their work *The German Ideology* Karl Marx and Frederick Engels point out, "The ideas of the ruling class are in every epoch the ruling ideas, i.e., the class which is the ruling material force of society is at the same time its ruling intellectual force." It is indisputable that the Medieval Church and the feudal lords, equally with their successors, the world capitalist class, bear responsibility for the perpetuation of anti-gay prejudices among the masses of people. The existence of specially oppressed groups, gays and others, has historically provided convenient scapegoats for deflecting the frustration and anger of the exploited masses away from the ruling classes. Unfortunately, sexual, racial and other forms of prejudice have often kept the masses divided and fighting among themselves.

While the genocidal campaigns against sexual heretics died out with the rise of the European bourgeoisie, the use of the charge of homosexuality against political enemies and other opponents remains a favored tactic among reactionaries to the present day, especially in the U.S. One need only recall the words of the district attorney at the Chicago 8 Conspiracy trial, who characterized the rebellious youth movement of the 1960s as the "Freaking Fag Revolution." Senator Joseph McCarthy, whose assignment in the early 1950s was to raise the anti-communist hysteria to a fever pitch, was almost as generous with his accusations of homosexuality as he was with his red-baiting. Unfortunately, the Stalinist bureaucracy in the Soviet Union stooped to the same kind of gay-baiting attacks against the Nazis and against political opponents at home. As terrible as this was, we will see in a later chapter that it does not really compare with the Nazi line on homosexuality, which was to re-introduce on a mass scale the extermination campaign that had died out with the decline of feudalism in Europe.

## LESBIAN AND GAY OPPRESSION UNDER CAPITALISM

The feudal system of production was, at first, very decentralized with each unit more or less self-contained. Each manor produced its own food, clothing and household implements. But as the system developed, the consequent enrichment of the petty lords was a profound stimulus to regional, continental and intercontinental trade. The towns gradually acquired more and more importance, first as centers of trade and handicraft production, later for the guild system of industrial production.

In competition with the closed and inefficient guild system, the wealthy merchants of the towns (the burghers or bourgeoisie) began setting up manufacturing enterprises of their own. These industries were worked by "free labor"—poor people, often runaway serfs, hired for a set wage. Production was broken down into a series of stages, each worker's labor confined to one stage, repeated over and over.

The guild system could not long survive in the face of such an efficient and more profitable alternative. The addition of steam power and continual improvements in machinery guaranteed the supremacy of early capitalism over feudalism.

Engels wrote, in his introduction to an early Italian edition of *The Communist Manifesto* : "The first capitalist nation was Italy. The close of the feudal Middle Ages, and the opening of the modern capitalist era are marked by a colossal figure: an Italian, Dante, both the last poet of the Middle Ages and the first poet of modern times." Dante's major work, *The Divine Comedy,* was in part an attack on the political tyranny and moral bankruptcy of the Catholic Church. The sentiments reflected in this work were held by an important section of the merchant and banking class of Florence and other

Italian cities who were growing strong enough to challenge the Church's domination of economic and political life.

In the course of Dante's long poem, the poet tours hell, purgatory and heaven. Surprisingly, it is in purgatory where Dante comes across two groups of homosexuals. They are being purified there in preparation for a heavenly afterlife in paradise. The relative moral leniency thus suggested—the Church, after all, held that homosexuals were doomed to eternal damnation—probably reflects the tendency in Italy at that time to ridicule and defy the Church's sexual hypocrisy. Boccaccio and other writers were quite open in their attacks against the Church's moral duplicity. Also, because of the enthusiasm with which the new bourgeoisie greeted their creations, many gay artists and artisans of the time were afforded a measure of freedom from persecution, protected as they were by their patrons. The presence of many open or semi-open gay people in the bourgeois art world up to the present day may well have something to do with this Renaissance precedent, a notable exception to the pervasive vilification of homosexuals.

## The Political Meaning of Sexual Repression Under Capitalism

By the time the Industrial Revolution had begun transforming the kingdoms of Europe into powerful industrial countries, the wild anti-woman and anti-homosexual persecutions instigated by the Catholic and Protestant Churches and perpetuated for centuries had subsided. But if the hysteria was gone, the prejudice itself was now woven into the very fabric of life. The sexual-religious cults of the peasants had been largely wiped out. The subjugation of women went almost unquestioned. Patriarchal Christianity reigned supreme.

The great bourgeois revolution in France at the end of the 18th century removed the vestiges of feudal power from French society. It was a profound social upheaval in which the oppressed masses of the cities played a very important role. The revolution signaled a radical break with the past. In the new legal code, called the Code Napoleon, homosexual acts were excluded from the list of offenses. Most of the other European nations followed suit in the succeeding decades. Great Britain, Germany and the United States did not.

From a class point of view, this movement away from the anti-homosexual hysteria must be seen as a recognition of bourgeois sexual rights by the political leaders of the young democratic bourgeoisie. Certainly in practice, though the degree and form of oppression have varied from country to country and from period to period, sexual rights have continued to be profoundly restricted for the masses of people. All the countries of the capitalist West have perpetuated the oppression of lesbian and gay people just as they have perpetuated, with and without the aid of law, the oppression and exploitation of women, Third World peoples, members of oppressed nationalities and working people in general.

Anti-gay prejudice is an instrument of bourgeois class rule, just as it was for the feudal rulers and just as national chauvinism, sexism and racism are. In the epoch of imperialist wars, proletarian revolutions and national liberation movements, the billionaire capitalist class uses every means at its disposal to divide the international working class. In addition to dividing straight from gay, anti-gay prejudice can be used to discredit straight people, who sometimes find it difficult to disprove allegations of homosexual acts. Sexual prejudices in general tend to make people feel defensive and guilty about themselves. Sexual prejudices breed confusion, frustration and fear. The great gay North American poet Walt Whitman, for example, found it necessary to protest in the strongest terms when he was questioned directly about the homoeroticism in his poem "Leaves of Grass."

## Capitalism—Its Basic Dynamics and Contradictions

Modern capitalism quickly proved its superiority over previous productive systems. Greed for greater and greater profits was and is its driving force. Especially in the pre-monopolistic period of capitalism, profit meant the ability to renew and modernize the physical equipment of production, to introduce technical money-saving innovations as they appeared. It meant the ability to expand production, a process that tended to cut the per-unit cost of manufactured products. Irrational expansion based solely on the desire for greater profits resulted, however, in cyclic periods of overproduction and depression when economic development came to a standstill.

As capitalism became monopolistic, these periodic convulsions intensified and became international in character, reflecting the profound tendency of capitalism to expand beyond national boundaries, to seek out new sources of raw materials, cheap labor, and markets for its products. By the time of World War I the capitalist countries of Europe and the U.S. had divided and enslaved almost the whole world among themselves. World War I was fought for no other reason than to redivide global economic resources. Germany lost not just the war but also its colonial empire and its world markets.

Marx was the first to show that every social formation contains the seeds of its own destruction. In this sense, the supreme creation of capitalism has been the great international working class. The capitalists in their constant drive for greater profits brought together thousands of people under one factory roof. Millions crowded together in the workers' quarters of European and U.S. industrial cities. Today this process continues to generate greater and greater numbers of workers, especially as the countries of Asia, Africa and Latin America become industrialized. The oppressed and exploited masses, fragmented and isolated from each other under feudalism, now come into daily contact with thousands of their brothers and sisters as the wage slaves of capitalism—the possessionless workers who sell the only thing they have, their labor power, to the capitalists for long periods each work day.

For the modern working class, the periodic convulsions of capitalist production along with the periodic imperialist wars of expansion are the source of truly catastrophic suffering. The conversation between the unemployed miner and his daughter tells it all:

> "Daddy, why is it so cold?"
> "Because there's no coal."
> "Why isn't there any coal?"
> "Because there's no work."
> "Why isn't there any work?"
> "Because there's too much coal."

As surely today as in earlier periods, international capitalism (imperialism) must continually expand production to ensure its survival. Yet, because production under capitalism is geared to profit rather than human need, a point is inevitably reached when more is produced than can be sold. There follows a period of economic collapse with widespread unemployment and impoverishment. Imperialism increasingly resorts to war and fascism to pull itself out of these declines.

This is the political background for two developments in capitalist Germany. We will first consider the development at the end of the 19th century of a homosexual rights movement, and second the development and temporary victory of the anti-gay forces of German fascism. We are indebted for much of the material on the homosexual rights movement in Germany to the work of gay researchers James Steakley, John Lauritsen and David Thorstad.

## The Dawning of Resistance to Gay Oppression

In his well-researched work *The Homosexual Emancipation Movement in Germany,* Canadian gay liberationist James Steakley traces the roots and development of a movement for homosexual rights in pre-Nazi Germany. Steakley notes that the first indications of a challenge to the prevailing anti-homosexual prejudice came in the 1860s. Jean Baptiste von Schweitzer, a lawyer who had joined the section of the German workers' movement under Ferdinand Lassalle's leadership in 1862, was charged, tried and convicted later in that year of a homosexual act in a city park. Under attack by a number of his comrades and other working-class leaders, Schweitzer was publicly defended by Lassalle. Lassalle's position was, "In the long run, sexual activity is a matter of taste and ought to be left up to each person, so long as he doesn't encroach upon someone else's interests." In 1867, after the death of Lassalle, Schweitzer became president of the Universal German Workingmen's Association, the organization Lassalle had founded.

Karl Ulrichs was a prolific German writer whose efforts on behalf of homosexual rights, though mainly literary, also included some courageous but unsuccessful efforts around 1866 to prevent the enactment of Prussian anti-homosexual legislation in other parts of Germany. He was sentenced to a year in prison for his efforts. Upon his release, he made a further political effort, addressing the Congress of German Jurists. His arguments were greeted with shock and anger, however, and Ulrichs returned to his writing. Several physicians also spoke out against the legal persecution of homosexuals at this time.

Nevertheless the harsh Prussian law against homosexual acts between men was extended to all of Germany in 1871. This new law, Paragraph 175, was a serious blow. It was 25 years before voices of protest again began to be raised. Even so, Steakley points out, "this decade witnessed the end of homosexual invisibility."

## The Birth of an Organization for Homosexual Rights

In 1896 a periodical directed at homosexuals appeared in Berlin. About the same time a study of homosexuality by Magnus Hirschfeld was published in Leipzig. In May of 1897 Hirschfeld, together with several friends, founded the Scientific Humanitarian Committee, an organization specifically dedicated to gay emancipation. This organization had as its primary focus the repeal of Paragraph 175. It also sought, through its publications and through public meetings and extensive speaking tours, to educate the general public on the issue of homosexuality and to encourage other gay people to join the struggle.

The Committee's main activity was a petition campaign directed against Paragraph 175. The petition set forth the scientific and humanitarian reasons for ending the legal sanctions against gays. The Committee's approach was to solicit the signatures of prominent people who would lend an air of authority and respectability to the movement. In 1898, with the signatures of 900 prominent doctors, lawyers, educators, and scientists, the Committee made its initial approach to the German Reichstag, the national legislature. They were firmly rebuffed. Only the great Social Democrat August Bebel spoke out in their behalf.

In 1905 the petition was again brought before the Reichstag during another debate on Paragraph 175. By now there were 5,000 signatures. Opposition to the abolition of the anti-homosexual law was led by the Center Party, a right-wing group strongly backed by the Catholic Church. Attempting to counter the arguments of the Social Democrat Adolph Thiele, who said, "For my part, I wouldn't even admit that this is something sick; it's simply a deviation from the usual pattern nature produces," a Center Party representative observed that although 5,000 people had signed the petition, the overwhelming majority of the population—60 million—had not. The move for reform was again defeated.

In their book *The Early Homosexual Rights Movement (1864-1935)* gay liberationists John Lauritsen and David Thorstad cite an attempt by Hirschfeld to determine the prevalence of homosexuality among male German students and workers. In an early use of the survey technique, questionnaires were sent to over 3,000 students and 6,000 metal workers. The results suggested to Hirschfeld that 2.2 percent of the population or 1,200,000 Germans were homosexual. Though the validity of the poll might be subject to serious question, it is certainly significant that none of the metal workers queried objected to the survey. On the other hand, a Protestant minister in league with six "insulted" students filed charges against Hirschfeld for "disseminating indecent writings". Lauritsen and Thorstad quote Hirschfeld speaking movingly in defense of his activities:

> I would feel that I had brought down blame upon myself were I, who possess the knowledge that I have accumulated in the field of homosexuality, not to do everything in my power to destroy an erroneous idea, the consequences of which human language is not rich enough to describe. At the beginning of this very week, a well-known homosexual student at the School of Technology poisoned himself because of his homosexuality. In my medical practice, I have at present a student in the same school who shot himself in the heart. Just a few weeks ago, in this very room, I attended a case against two blackmailers who had driven a homosexual gentleman—one of the most honorable men whom I knew—to suicide—something a second individual, pursued by the same blackmailers, could only with difficulty be dissuaded from doing. I could present hundreds of cases like this, and others similar to it. I felt it was necessary to bring about this inquiry in order to free humanity of a blemish that it will some day think back on with the deepest sense of shame.

Hirschfeld was found guilty and fined 200 Marks.

In 1909, Germany was at the height of an anti-gay panic precipitated by the exposure several years earlier of alleged homosexual activities of a number of high German political figures. The Reichstag began consideration of a proposal to extend Paragraph 175 to include homosexual acts between women. Although a number of women had played an active role in the Scientific Humanitarian Committee from 1901 on, the struggle against this new attack on sexual rights brought many more women into the movement. Left and bourgeois women's groups that had previously avoided the issue of lesbianism now mobilized in defense of the rights of homosexual women and men.

## The Left Tradition of Support for Gay and Lesbian Rights

The outbreak of World War I brought a temporary halt to the struggle. It also precipitated a profound split in the international working-class movement. The German Social Democrats were a powerful and revolutionary workers' party previous to the war. This party in turn belonged to the Second International, the dynamic Marxist organization composed of working class leaders and workers' groups in many countries. The Social Democrats, before the formation of the German Communist Party, provided almost the only political support for the homosexual emancipation movement in Germany.

As early as 1895 the Social Democrats showed some responsiveness to the question of gay rights. Eduard Bernstein, an important leader of the Party, wrote in defense of the British literary figure Oscar Wilde in Die Neue Zeit, the principal organ of the Second International in Germany. Wilde had just been arrested and charged with "sodomy." Bernstein's was practically the only voice in Germany to speak out on Wilde's behalf. Lauritsen and Thorstad report that Bernstein's article called on the Social Democratic Party to lead the way in sexual reform, challenged the prevailing prejudice against lesbians and gays, and rejected the psychiatric theories about homosexuality that were just then coming into vogue. In Britain, where homosexual acts between men had remained punishable by death until 1861 and remained illegal until 1967, Wilde was tried and convicted by the press as well as the court. He was sent to prison for three years. Panic spread among England's gay population. Incidentally, Wilde was the only British literary figure of the time willing to sign a petition in support of the Haymarket martyrs in the U.S. He died a few years after his release from prison.

With the development of the struggle against Paragraph 175, Social Democratic leaders took the floor of the Reichstag to argue in defense of homosexual rights each time the petition was introduced. Hirschfeld himself was affiliated with the Social Democratic Party from 1898 until he left Germany just before the Nazi takeover.

In its early period the Social Democratic movement was truly revolutionary and continued the work to build an international workers' movement that had been begun by Marx and Engels. With the outbreak of World War I, however, German Social Democrats broke decisively with the movement for proletarian internationalism by siding with their own bourgeoisie, the German capitalist class, in support of the imperialist war. Karl Leibknecht and Rosa Luxembourg were the only Social Democratic leaders in Germany to take the revolutionary position of the Russian Social Democratic leaders, Lenin and Trotsky, that working people of the various capitalist countries should not fight and kill each other in a war for capitalist profits. "Turn the imperialist war into a civil war! Don't shoot your working class brothers! Turn your guns around, against your capitalist oppressors!" This was the position of those working-class leaders who really understood how to overthrow the oppressive rule of capitalism.

And this program was carried out in Russia. The Bolsheviks, the left wing of the Social Democratic Party in Russia, led the Russian workers, soldiers and peasants to a seizure of state power in October 1917.

class collaboration with the German bourgeoisie. As a direct result of the Bolshevik Revolution in Russia, militant working-class leaders in Germany and many other countries left the Social Democratic Parties and organized Communist Parties in their respective countries. These new parties were united by the Third International, under the leadership of Lenin and Trotsky, until Lenin's death in 1924.

## Communist Support and Nazi Malevolence

In Germany the Communist Party quickly became influential. It responded, as the Social Democratic Party had previously, to the call for support against Paragraph 175. Felix Halle was a communist lawyer who worked with Kurt Hiller, an important leader of the Scientific Humanitarian Committee in the 1920s, on legislation for sexual reform. Halle wrote the following as a clarification of the German Communist Party's position on homosexuality:

> The class-conscious proletariat, uninfluenced by the ideology of property and freed from the ideology of the churches, approaches the question of sex life and also the problem of homosexuality with a lack of prejudice afforded by an understanding of the overall social structure. ... In accordance with the scientific insights of modern times, the proletariat regards these relations as a special form of sexual gratification and demands the same freedom and restrictions for these forms of sex life as for intercourse between the sexes, i.e., protection of the sexually immature from attacks, ... control over one's own body, and finally respect for the rights of non-involved parties.

In 1928 Adolf Brand, a founding member of an elitist and male chauvinist German gay group called the Community of the Special, polled the political parties of Germany on their positions with regard to the reform of Paragraph 175. The Communist Party replied:

> The CP has ... taken a stand for the repeal of Paragraph 175 at every available opportunity. We need simply remind you of the recent [Reichstag] debate on the law for fighting venereal disease as well as the debate of the [Reichstag] Committee for Penal Code Reform. There is no need to emphasize that we will continue to wage the most resolute struggle for the repeal of these laws in the future.

The National Socialist German Labor Party, the Nazis, answered Brand's query with the following words:

> It is not necessary that you and I live, but it is necessary that the German people live. And it can only live if it can fight, for life means fighting. And it can only fight if it maintains its masculinity. It can only maintain its masculinity if it exercises discipline, especially in matters of love. Free love and deviance are undisciplined. Therefore we reject you, as we reject anything which hurts our people.
>
> Anyone who even thinks of homosexual love is our enemy. We reject anything which emasculates our people and makes it a plaything for our enemies, for we know that life is a fight and it's madness to think that men will ever embrace fraternally. Natural history teaches the opposite. Might makes right. And the stronger will always win over the weak. Let's see to it that we once again become the strong! But this we can only do in one way—the German people must once again learn to exercise discipline. We therefore reject any form of lewdness, especially homosexuality, because it robs us of our last chance to free our people from the bondage which now enslaves it.

The appearance and growth of the Nazi Party was a result of the inability of German capitalism to recover from the losses it had suffered in World War I. The Nazis organized among the most backward elements of society, using the most disgusting racial and sexual prejudices to play on the anger, frustrations, and ignorance of financially failing sections of the petty bourgeoisie. They were especially successful among the ruined petty bourgeois elements, the shopkeepers, landlords, managers and others who had, in more prosperous times, lived higher than the working people and looked down on them. Now when times were bad the Nazis said the Jews and Communists were the cause of it. Maybe the fascists could put the country back together and restore prosperity.

The Nazis also spouted anti-capitalist rhetoric. But this was only a cover for their real role as shock troops for the German capitalists, and reflected the extreme hostility toward the rich that existed everywhere. In reality, the Nazis were financed by the bankers and big industrialists who sought to destroy the powerful left parties and the trade union movement and consciously utilized the Nazis to this end.

As is clear from their statement in reply to Adolf Brand, the Nazis were strongly opposed to homosexuality. Hirschfeld, who was gay, a transvestite and of Jewish background, was a perfect target for them. In 1920 Nazis physically attacked a meeting at which Hirschfeld was speaking in Munich. Hirschfeld was beaten. In 1921 Hirschfeld was again attacked in Munich by fascists. His skull was fractured and he was left for dead. In 1923 a meeting at which he was speaking in Vienna was attacked by young Nazis who first hurled stink bombs to create a panic and then opened fire on the audience. Several people were wounded though Hirschfeld himself was not hurt. The Munich chapter of the German Friendship Association, another gay organization of this period, was forced to disband by constant Nazi harassment.

**Hirschfeld Becomes Demoralized**

The German homosexual rights movement was basically petty bourgeois in its class character. It had no strong roots in the working class, though, as we have noted, it received support from the major German workers' parties. Hirschfeld himself appears to have become demoralized in the 1920s and by 1925 the leadership of the Scientific Humanitarian Committee was largely in the hands of Kurt Hiller, whose orientation was even more academic and legalistic than Hirschfeld's. In 1927 Hirschfeld made an evaluation of the homosexual movement which included the following words:

> Aside from a few minor cliques, homosexuals are almost totally lacking in feelings of solidarity; in fact, it would be difficult to find another class of mankind which has proved so incapable of organizing to secure its basic legal and human rights.

Such a statement, though clearly spoken in frustration and demoralization, reveals a profound ignorance of the effects of oppression and the psychology of oppressed people. Hirschfeld, though providing an inspiring example of dedication and self-sacrifice, had never taken up the challenge of mass struggle. Rather than directing his efforts toward the gay and straight working masses, the class with the real potential to transform society, he concentrated on the privileged, the influential, and the powerful—those with the most to lose from any real social change. The bone-deep feeling of solidarity that arises from mass struggle, this the oppressed lesbians and gay men of Germany never felt. In great meassure their leaders were responsible for this. They seem to have preferred drawing rooms and legislative chambers to the streets and meeting places of the working class districts.

## The Struggle Against Fascism and Its Betrayeal

The victory of fascism in Germany was not inevitable. The working-class movement there was extremely large, though divided in half by the Social Democrats and Communists who were mutually hostile. As the social crisis deepened through the 1920s, the capitalists more and more made use of Nazi goon squads and paramilitary units against workers' meetings, the workers' press, and working-class leaders. Members of the left wing of the workers' movement, many of whom identified with the Left Opposition in the Soviet Union, saw the need for unity between the Social Democratic Party and the Communist Party on the issue of fighting fascism. They understood a fact that the others, in their factional blindness, missed: The struggle against fascism was a fight to the death.

The Third International after Lenin had been transformed by Stalin into an instrument of Soviet foreign policy. Stalin and the bureaucratic grouping that rose to power with him were frightened by the international class struggle. They themselves had attained a measure of comfort and privilege behind the backs of the revolutionary Russian masses who were exhausted, impoverished and bereft of many of their most talented and dedicated fighters as a result of the unsuccessful imperialist invasion of Russia and the civil war that followed the Bolshevik revolution.

The Stalinist bureaucracy sought accommodation with the capitalist leaders of the West. It also underestimated the meaning of fascism and went so far as to characterize the German Social Democratic Party rather than the Nazis as the real enemy. With the ranks of the workers so horribly divided the Nazis were victorious.

## With the Fascist Victory Came an
## Anti-Gay Extermination Campaign

Many people have a serious misconception about the position of the Nazi regime on the issue of homosexuality. This has a lot to do with the fact that before and during World War II, the other imperialist powers—and also, unfortunately, the Soviet government—gay-baited the Nazi regime as part of their ideological offensive against it. But the Nazis gay-baited back and went far beyond verbal abuse in their treatment of gays and lesbians unfortunate enough to be living under their rule.

We have seen how quickly the new Bolshevik government had acted on the issue of homosexuality. After their consolidation of power in early 1933, the Nazis acted quickly, too—in their own way. Following James Steakley's account:

> Kurt Hiller's apartment was invaded and searched by the SS on March 7, and he was eventually sent to the concentration camp at Oranienburg. ... On May 6, a Berlin newspaper announced that the city was to be purged of un-German spirit by destroying objectionable books. The first target of this campaign was Hirschfeld's Institute for Sexual Science, described by the Nazis as "the international center of the white slave trade" and "an unparalleled breeding ground of dirt and filth."

To the accompaniment of a brass band, Nazi students invaded the building, which also housed the offices of the Scientific Humanitarian Committee. They carted out more than 12,000 books, a large and valuable picture file, unpublished manuscripts and important records. All this material was burned in a public ceremony on May 10. A bust of Hirschfeld was first carried through the streets in a Nazi torchlight procession and then thrown into the fire of burning books. Hirschfeld had left Germany for a far-ranging tour in 1930 and wisely did not return. He died in French exile in 1935.

Ernest Roehm was a more or less openly gay Nazi who played an important role in Hitler's rise to power. Roehm and many of his closest SA associates were murdered on June 28, 1934, in a political maneuver Hitler himself engineered to increase his own power. As a cover, Hitler and the other Nazi leaders pointed to the homosexual activities of Roehm and other SA officers as the reason for the "Night of the Long Knives" massacre. At the same time the massacre was being organized, the same day in fact, Hitler issued the following order to SA:

I expect all SA leaders to help to preserve and strengthen the SA in its capacity as a pure and cleanly institution. In particular, I should like every mother to be able to allow her son to join the SA, Party and Hitler Youth without fear that he may become morally corrupted in their ranks. I therefore required all SA commanders to take utmost pains to ensure that offences under Paragraph 175 are met by immediate expulsion of the culprit from the SA and Party.

A year later the Nazis amended Paragraph 175 to include kisses, embraces and even homosexual fantasies as punishable offenses. Prosecutions based on this infamous law increased 900 percent after the purge of Roehm, from about 3,000 prosecutions between 1931 and 1934 to almost 30,000 between 1936 and 1939.

Opposition to homosexuality assumed a fanatical character among the ranks of the Nazi leaders. Hans Bleuel reports some of their statements on the subject in his book *Sex and Society in Nazi Germany*. Reich Legal Director Hans Frank, for example, believed: "Homosexual activity means the negation of the community as it must be constituted if the race is not to perish. That is why homosexual behavior, in particular, merits no mercy." Gestapo leader Heinrich Himmler had the following to say: "We can't permit such a danger to the country; the homosexuals must be entirely eliminated."

Himmler is also reported to have favored castration as a "cure" for male homosexuality, although not to the exclusion of execution. He issued the following order regarding gay offenders in the SS: "After serving the sentence imposed by the court, they will, on my instructions, be taken to a concentration camp and there shot while attempting to escape."

Although the Nazis used the charge of homosexuality hypocritically against both homosexuals and heterosexuals, there is no question but that their goal was the total extermination of all identifiable gay people. Estimates of the number of gays who were executed or died in the concentration camps range into the hundreds of thousands; 220,000 is the estimate recently made by the Protestant Church of Austria. They were confined to the Level III camps, the "mills of death" that few people survived. And they were stigmatized by a pink triangle worn on the left side of the jacket and the right pant leg.

The following firsthand accounts from James Steakley's book graphically illustrate the anti-gay nightmare the Nazis created:

> The homosexuals were grouped into liquidation commandos and placed under triple camp discipline. That meant less food, more work, stricter supervision. If a prisoner with a pink triangle became sick, it spelled his doom. Admission to the clinic was forbidden.
>
> The escapees had been brought back. "Homo" was scrawled scornfully across their clothing for their last march through the camp. To increase their thirst, they were forced to eat oversalted food, and then they were placed on the block and whipped. Afterwards, drums were hung around their necks, which they beat while shouting, "Hurrah, we're back!" The three men were hanged.
>
> Since they could not or would not give up their vice, they knew they would never be released. This extremely powerful psychological factor hastened the physical collapse of these individuals. ... If one lost his "friend" through sickness or death, you could see it was all over. Many committed suicide. The "friend" meant everything to these creatures in this situation. On several occasions two friends committed suicide together.

The following passage from Eugen Kogon's book *The Theory and Practice of Hell* clearly illustrates the Nazis' "final solution" to the gay question and, in political terms that have even greater meaning today, the murderous character of monopoly capitalism in its period of decline:

> Until the fall of 1938 the homosexuals in Buchenwald were divided up among the barracks occupied by political prisoners, where they led a rather inconspicuous life. In October 1938, they were transferred to the penal company in a body and had to slave in the quarry. This consigned them to the lowest caste in camp during the most difficult years. In shipments to extermination camps, such as Nordhausen, Natzweiler and Gross-Rosen, they furnished the highest proportionate share, for the camp had an understandable tendency to slough off all elements considered least valuable or worthless. If anything could save them at all, it was to enter into sordid relationships within the camp, but this was as likely to endanger their lives as to save them. Theirs was an insoluble predicament and virtually all of them perished.

Just like the Jews, the Gypsies and the working-class leaders, the gays of Nazi Germany were made scapegoats for the crisis of German capitalist society.

## The Real Heirs to the Nazi Tradition

It is most unfortunate that the capitalist class of the U.S. has succeeded to a great extent in its propaganda effort to link the political opposites of fascism and communism in many people's minds. Certainly the material in this chapter and the last gives no support to such a position. And if there are governments in the world today that bear striking resemblances to the Nazi creation, they are not to be found in the ranks of the socialist camp. The fascist regimes in Turkey, Indonesia and south Korea, to name some of the worst, are all creations of the U.S., set up by the CIA in cooperation with puppet military leaders, most of whom were originally trained by the Pentagon.

It was the racist U.S. government itself that used the atom bomb against the working-class cities of Hiroshima and Nagasaki when it was already certain that Japan was going to surrender. It was the big business-controlled government of the U.S. that invaded Korea in 1950, attempted genocide against the Vietnamese in the 1960s and early 1970s, and has arrogantly delegated to itself the right to install puppet governments all across the globe. And it is the U.S. that holds captive the Black, Latin, Native and Asian nations within its own borders, that super-exploits and super-oppresses them, finding them useful as sources of cheap labor when times are good and expendable scapegoats in times of economic crisis.

No country in the world today has an adequate position with regard to ending the oppression of lesbians, gay men and transgendered people. But to single out any socialist country for special attack, as some in the U.S. have done, is to cover over this important fact. In addition, it lets the U.S. imperialists—the ones who have a real stake in maintaining racism, sexism, and lesbian/gay oppression—off the hook.

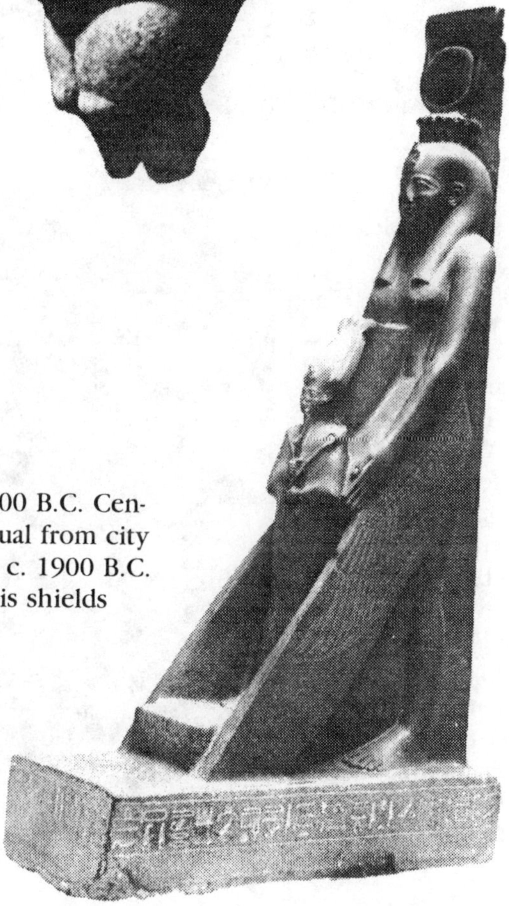

Top, goddess figure, c. 25,000 B.C. Center, iImage of lesbian sex ritual from city of Ur (in what is now Iraq), c. 1900 B.C. Bottom, Egyptian goddess Isis shields god Osiris, c. 600 B.C.

Top: London statue of legendary warrior queen Boadicea, who led resistance to Roman invaders in the first century A.D. Some researchers believe the slang epithet "bulldyke" is derived from her name. Bottom: Joan of Arc, in battle garb on dark horse. From a 15th-century German tapestry.

Top, ceremony honoring berdache, Sauk and Fox nations, 19th century, as depicted by artist George Catlin. Bottom, berdache slaughtered by European invaders. 16th-century engraving.

Right: Amazon warriors of Dahomey, Africa, 19th century.

Left: Nazis carrying bust of Magnus Hirschfeld to throw into a fire of burning books, 1933.

Right: Navy "war council," including Franklin Roosevelt (third from left) planned post-World War I witchhunt against gay sailors.

Top left: Wyoming miners dance at an all-male ball, 1880s. Top right: a lesbian couple, 1930. Bottom right: Oscar Wilde.

Top, the first Gay Pride march, June 1970. Center, youths gather outside the Stonewall Inn during the week of the rebellion, June 1969. Bottom, 1971 demonstration.

Top, Gay Pride Day, 1976. Bottom, blocking filming of the anti-gay movie "Cruising," 1976.

Top, Gay Pride, 1977. Center, first national march, 1979. Bottom, Marsha Johnson, a founder of Street Transvestite Action Revolutionaries. Johnson was murdered in 1992, another victim of violence against gays and transgendered people.

Top, groups like Jerry Falwell's "Moral Majority" made the lesbian and gay community a major target of the religious right wing in the 1980s. Bottom, marching against racist and anti-gay police violence, 1982.

Top: Rage at 1986 Supreme Court ruling upholding "sodomy" laws. Right: The Names Project quilt honoring people who've died of AIDS. Left: It took eight years of struggle to win a disabled lesbian's right to be with her lover.

Top: Workers World Party contingent, Lesbian and Gay Pride Day 1987. Author Bob McCubbin, in cap, holds banner at center. Bottom: Trade union support for lesbian and gay struggle is growing.

Top: Sgt. Perry Watkins, a gay transvestite, fought his discharge from the U.S. Army. The Pentagon drafted him during the Vietnam war, then booted him out afterward. Bottom: The AIDS activist movement took to the streets to protest government indifference to the epidemic.

Top: AIDS protest in 1988. The older man in the center is Harry Hay, one of the founders of the modern lesbian and gay movement. Bottom: The AIDS Coalition to Unleash Power—ACT UP—decried the 1991 U.S. war against Iraq, demanding funding for health care, not warfare.

San Francisco's streets erupted when California's governor vetoed a gay rights bill in 1991. Sign here reads: "Pete Wilson is a liar. He discriminates against minorities. Who will be next?"

Top: 1991 international lesbian and gay conference, Acapulco, Mexico.
Bottom: Lesbian and gay youths protest police brutality.

"Domestic partner" laws recognizing same-sex couples—in some cases symbolically, in others with concrete marriage-equivalent benefits—are in effect in several cities. Here, a gay couple brings their son to see them register as domestic partners, 1993.

## Lesbian and Gay Oppression in the U.S.

We have tried to show through the historical outline in the preceding chapters that the hostility to homosexuality that exists throughout Western capitalist society is not part of the "natural order" of things, but rather developed after the world historic overthrow of matriarchal society. We have suggested that the new sexual restrictions were based on the need for undisputed paternity to determine heirs. The oppressing function that religion assumed with the rise of social classes formalized and made use of these new restrictions. As patriarchal monotheistic religions replaced earlier forms, sexuality—and especially homosexuality—came under increasing attack.

Under the leadership of the medieval Catholic Church, anti-homosexual frenzy reached a frenzied and murderous peak. This panic was also manifested in various Protestant movements, some of which were equally zealous in their persecutions of all manifestations of sexual expression outside monogamous heterosexual marriage. The wild character of the prejudice appears to have subsided as a result of the increasing secularization of society that accompanied the development of capitalism. Nevertheless, the basic prejudice was preserved and has continued to serve as a powerful weapon of social coercion, division, confusion—and not infrequently, outright terror against the masses of people.

The German Nazi regime made full use of homophobia as well as racism, sexism, and national chauvinism in its efforts to destroy all resistance to capitalist rule and imperialist adventures. Shortly after the CIA-sponsored counter-revolution in Chile in 1973, the new fascist military rulers there began an extermination campaign against Chilean gay people. Although the reports were sketchy in the face of the overwhelming repression against all progressive forces and the whole Chilean working class and peasantry, a number of facts concerning the anti-gay terror there emerged.

President Allende, who was murdered by the fascists during the takeover, and other leaders of the Popular Unity government and the progressive forces were repeatedly gay-baited by the fascists. In the first days of the Pinochet regime, fascist troops marched through the streets of Santiago chanting, "Death to the faggots!" On-the-scene observers reported the deaths of many gays whose bodies were left lying in the streets as part of the campaign to sow terror among the revolutionary masses.

## The Lesbian and Gay Community in the U.S.— A History of Bloody Oppression

In the U.S., fear and hostility toward homosexuality have always been the norm. The early Puritan colonists were among the most fiercely anti-sexual of the Protestant sects and they raged uncontested in a number of the English settlements in North America. In 1642 the Puritan governor of Plymouth, William Bradford, assessed the persistence of "sin" in his colony despite the most brutal attempts—including death by burning at the stake—to suppress it: "...not only incontinencie between persons unmarried ... but that which is even worse, even sodomie and bugerie (things fearfull to name), have brook forth in this land, oftener than once." Even in the colonies not dominated by Puritans, death was a common punishment for homosexuality.

In more recent times, homosexuality has lost none of its potential for provoking the most brutal and sometimes murderous responses. On a spring evening in 1961 a young man named William Hall stood waiting for a trolley near his home in San Francisco. A short while later he was dead, the victim of a gang of hoodlums who decided to kill him when he answered their question, "Are you a queer?" with one of his own, "What if I asked you that question?"

In the summer of 1971 a group of lesbians and gay men attempted to have a picnic for themselves in a public park in Bridgeport, Connecticut. Their presence infuriated a nearby group of straight people who attacked and beat them. One of the lesbians, seriously injured by the blows of the bigots, staggered from the park and requested the aid of a passing cop. "Aid" came—in the form of arrests—of the gay people!

In the summer of 1973, two young men standing in front of a gay bar in Boston were invited to "a party" by six other young men. Instead of a party, they were taken to a deserted park, beaten, stabbed, robbed, and stuffed into a sewer. One of them died.

Most acts of brutality against lesbians, gay men and transgendered people never make the newspapers, and when they do, it often takes reading between the lines to figure out the truth. Except when the attacker is brought to trial, most cases of anti-gay violence, even murder, are not even reported as such. And with astonishing frequency, judges consider the argument of defense against a homosexual overture by an older man to justify murder in these cases. Possible "corruption of youth" apparently is a more serious offense than murder in their eyes.

Transvestites are particularly frequent targets of murderous assaults. In November of 1970 a Black transvestite named James Clay was murdered by Chicago cops who shot him eight times in the back. The cops, one of whom knew Clay and had arrested him previously, said the shots were fired "to prevent his escape." And from the New York Times of November 25, 1973: "A South Bronx man died yesterday several hours after he was set upon near his home by a gang of a dozen youths who beat and sexually mutilated him. Detectives identified the victim as William Battles, 31 years old ... and said he was wearing women's clothes when he was attacked." A young transvestite named James Arcuri was stabbed to death on a street in Greenwich Village in August 1975. A police description of the victim said he "was dressed in a skirt, blouse and tall platform heels" and had been stabbed after he responded to the insult of a passerby.

## Anti-Gay/Lesbian Persecution at Home and on the Job

Most lesbians and gay men are invisible in the sense that they are able to pass as heterosexuals in their everyday public lives. While this "passing" has had the harmful effect of allowing the traditional anti-gay stereotypes to continue unchallenged, it is a matter of survival for many lesbian and gay working people. Even today, in most areas of the country, bosses and landlords have a free hand with gay workers and tenants they want to get rid of.

Except for in a few dozen cities and six states that have passed lesbian/gay civil rights legislation, gay people who are fired or refused jobs or apartments for being gay have no legal recourse. "Sodomy" laws making homosexuality a crime are still on the books in 24 states. And even where laws protecting gay people have recently been enacted, the situation is comparable to the position of Black people following the civil rights legislation of the 1960s. Formal equality in law is often only a meassure of the distance between what should be and the discrimination that continues to exist with or without legal sanction.

In 1972, Peggy Burton was dismissed from her high school teaching position in Oregon because of rumors that she was a lesbian. The principal's action was then affirmed by a school board ruling. Burton, who openly admitted her sexual orientation, was given no opportunity to defend herself. She then won a suit against the school board for back pay but was denied the right to reinstatement. Burton's students didn't need a court ruling to see on which side justice lay. The graduating class where she taught dedicated their yearbook to her and added the motto: "Prejudice is the child of ignorance." The district school superintendent then had the dedication page torn out of each yearbook and destroyed!

Many gay people have had experiences like that of Anna Marie Nunes, who was fired from Hughes Aircraft in 1971 when a routine security investigation uncovered the fact that she was a lesbian. The official reason given for firing her was falsification of the job application—but if she had told the truth she wouldn't have been hired in the first place.

Gay-baiting is a frequent tactic bosses use to divide workers and isolate potential leaders. In 1970 a militant though mild-mannered steel worker was running for shop steward in Buffalo's huge Bethlehem Steel Plant. Supervisors attempted to undermine the wide respect and support he enjoyed by starting a whispering campaign against him, alleging he was "queer." Rather than deny the rumor, the militant simply said his sexual orientation was irrelevant to the issue of how well he could represent the workers in his area of the plant. He went on to win the election.

Similar company-instigated gay-baiting occurred in 1974 in a New York City telephone office where women workers were organizing to throw out a company union and gain a real one. In this case, the attack was easier to fight, since there were a number of open lesbians in the office. When the union organizers, who were straight women, explained why the supervisors were spreading the rumor, it immediately heightened the class consciousness and solidarity of all the women in the office, lesbian and straight, and increased their determination to fight the bosses.

Gay parents, especially lesbians with children, are sometimes faced with a particularly cruel manifestation of oppression. There are many instances of lesbians being declared "unfit mothers" by the courts merely on the basis of their sexual orientation. Thus, what are usually very close and loving family units of one or two women and their children are callously ripped apart when brought to the attention of the courts. In 1974 a California court ordered a Los Angeles woman named Lynda Chaffin was to give up her 11- and 13-year-old daughters after she admitted to her parents that she was a lesbian. Chaffin refused and was forced into hiding with her children while her lawyer attempted to appeal the decision. Early in 1975 federal marshals located her on the basis of a fugitive-from-justice warrant. Though the charge was dropped when she turned herself in, her children were taken from her and she faced a long and expensive legal battle to even have the possibility of ever seeing them again.

## Lesbian and Gay Oppression in Military Life and in Prison

Lesbians and gay men are drawn to the U.S. military for many of the same reasons that heterosexual women and men are. For one thing, unemployment is a chronic feature of U.S. society and military advertisements aimed at working-class young people play up the mostly false image of the military as a place to learn practical job skills. The idea of "serving your country" is also drummed into the heads of young people from a very early age.

Military life is often a nightmare for gay people, however, and especially for lesbians. In their book *Lesbian/Woman* lesbian activists Del Martin and Phyllis Lyon describe the main features of the periodic purges that sweep through the women's quarters of U.S. military bases:

> For those who are not familiar with the mechanics of a "purge", it goes something like this. The armed forces are aware that despite careful screening, a certain percentage of all the women entering the service will have "homosexual tendencies." The purges are conducted by the male investigative agencies. ... Although the claim is that investigations are only made when there is a complaint, experience indicates that, like police, each base commander has a quota to meet. It usually begins by apprehending some youngster, new to the service and unaware of her rights, and scaring her into cooperation by threats and other third degree tactics. Interrogators usually inform her they will let her off if she will just give them names of other Lesbians. This constitutes the "complaint" necessary to launch a full-scale witch hunt which drives through a base relentlessly until a quota is filled.

Martin and Lyon talked with a number of women caught up in such purges who didn't even know what lesbianism was at the time they were charged with it.

Among men in the military, and also in prison, the sexual tensions that grow out of isolation from women and constant close contact with other men lead to a high incidence of homosexual activity. But besides the problem of persecution by military and prison authorities, there is another dangerous factor in these situations. Men who consider themselves heterosexual often find homosexual feelings very threatening. Their fear and frustration often find expression in anger directed at gay men. There is also the problem in prison of rape. Gay men in prison are sometimes forced into humiliating roles as the servants of bullies or agents of the warden. But the motive is often sheer survival under conditions of the constant threat of rape and beatings.

Other gay prisoners, who have taken up political struggles against their oppression and the inhuman system that calls their love illegal, are victims of official and unofficial attempts to silence them, sometimes by murder. Ernest Valenzuela, a Pima Indian, was one such victim. Valenzuela was a leading member of the North American Indian Cultural Group at the U.S. penitentiary at Leavenworth, Kansas, and was secretary and vice chair of the National Gay Prisoners Coalition. He was sent to solitary confinement many times for standing up for the rights and dignity of other prisoners.

On November 8, 1973, Valenzuela was set up and fatally stabbed by "unknown" assailants. He was denied access to the prison hospital until he was already dead. His friend John Gibbs and other brave gays in prisons across the country have refused to be intimidated by this and other acts of brutality, and are very much a part of the struggle against the U.S. concentration camp system.

To give an idea of what their captors, the officials who run the system, are like, it is only necessary to quote briefly from the writing of a former warden of San Quentin Prison, Clinton T. Duffy. In his book *Sex and Crime,* Duffy propounds the idea that sexual "deviation" is at the root of most "criminal" activity:

> In all the cases I've known, the deviation, not the felony, was the basic problem. If these people hadn't been homosexuals, they wouldn't have been felons. ...
>
> I am as sorry for the homosexual as for any other handicapped person, but I think we are now beginning to carry our sympathy for him a trifle too far. The tendency seems to be to try to justify him, to apologize for him, to accept him as he is, to let him along as he goes off on his own peculiar tangents. ...
>
> All convicts are potential homosexuals. And most homosexuals are potential convicts. I knew hundreds of them in my years at San Quentin and with the Adult Authority. ...

Former Warden Duffy is also an advocate of castration as a "cure" for crime and for homosexuality. He is not untypical of the sort of people who oversee the U.S. prison system as evidenced by the widespread use of cruel, unusual and truly monstrous practices against prisoners. Don Jackson, a gay activist who has written extensively about the Nazi-like prison conditions in California, has documented the use of castration against gay prisoners serving indeterminate sentences, although figures on the extent of this practice are kept secret.

Other barbaric practices, such as lobotomy and other forms of psycho-surgery, electro-shock, chemo-shock, and behavior modification, have been used against gay and straight prisoners at Vacaville State Prison and at Atascadero State Hospital, a maximum-security facility in California where sexual "criminals" and political prisoners are sent in hope of breaking their will to struggle. Though most fully documented in the California prison system, these practices exist in a number of other states and in the federal prison system also.

## The Political Use of Gay-Baiting

The use of gay-baiting in political struggles in the U.S. dates back at least to the heyday of Senator Joseph McCarthy, and probably goes back much further than that. McCarthy came close to equating the terms "homosexual" and "communist," as have fascists in other countries at other times. His wild accusations included the charge that President Truman was part of a communist conspiracy. While he eventually brought about his own downfall, his nationally televised inquisitorial hearings set a tone of suspicion and fear that pervaded all areas of U.S. life and lasted into the early 1960s.

In this national climate of reaction city officials in Boise, Idaho, launched an anti-gay crusade that was to disrupt the lives of hundreds of Boise residents before it subsided. This campaign, which began in 1955 and lasted almost a year, was researched a decade later by John Gerassi, who published his findings in a book called *The Boys of Boise*.

The anti-gay crusade began with the arrest of three men accused of having seduced two young boys. The "young boys" were actually rather worldly teenage hustlers who had eagerly accepted money from any number of adult gay men in Boise in return for "favors." Within nine days of the first arrests, one of those arrested had been sentenced to life imprisonment. More arrests followed, including charges against business and political leaders. Local newspaper accounts took on a wildly anti-gay character and in December it became national news when Time magazine proclaimed that Boise was the center of a national homosexual underworld that was corrupting young men by the hundreds. Rumors flew, neighbors denounced each other and men became afraid to go anywhere without their wives for fear of raising suspicions.

A decade later Gerassi was able to uncover the political power play that lay beneath the anti-gay panic: Two rival groups of political and business interests were locked in struggle in Idaho, and the leaders of one of these groups had launched the anti-gay campaign in an attempt to ensnare the leader of the other group, a politically powerful and wealthy man who was gay. The plan failed because the police refused to arrest this man although they were perfectly willing to ruin the lives of many less wealthy men. But the poisoned climate of fear still existed 10 years later when Gerassi visited Boise in the course of his research.

A later example of the bourgeois technique of gay-baiting comes from an October 1975 report in the Washington Post:

> A former senior Pentagon investigator said last week he was once ordered to "establish" that syndicated columnist Jack Anderson had a homosexual relationship with a suspected news source even though there was no reason to believe that one existed.
>
> W. Donald Stewart, who was in charge of an investigation into news leaks in late 1971, said the order was given to him by David Young, the Nixon Administration official in charge of the "Plumbers". ...
>
> Stewart said that Young got very upset when he refused the order. "This came from the President" Stewart quoted Young as saying, "It's the President's order."

# THE STRUGGLE THAT WILL END LESBIAN AND GAY OPPRESSION

The lesbian and gay liberation movement in the U.S. began, of course, with the Stonewall Rebellion in late June of 1969. But it should not be forgotten that previous to the Stonewall Rebellion there were a number of brave individuals and small so-called homophile organizations in the U.S. that spoke out for gay rights and dignity to one extent or another.

As early as 1924 an attempt was made to set up a gay organization in the U.S. modeled after the German Scientific Humanitarian Committee. The effort was unsuccessful, however. In 1948 a gay man named Henry Hay raised the idea of a gay men's organization to help in the campaign of Henry Wallace, a progressive candidate running for president against Truman and Dewey. He suggested the name "Bachelors for Wallace" but was unable to generate interest or support. In the middle 1950s, however, two organizations came into being: the Mattachine Society and the Daughters of Bilitis, which attempted to organize and aid, respectively, gay men and lesbians. These two organizations still exist.

There are also reports from the late 1950s and early 1960s of a number of lesbians and gay men, Black and white, who took active and leading roles in the Black civil rights struggle of that period, both in some northern cities and in the South. Of course, this was a time when an admission of homosexuality was tantamount to social suicide, even in most progressive circles. So the stories of these brave individuals are mostly unrecorded, as are the lives of the many progressive lesbian and gay people who participated in the labor struggles of the 1940s, the 1930s and earlier periods.

The lesbian and gay liberation movement, at least in its initial stages, was a profoundly militant, even revolutionary, movement.

The Stonewall Rebellion itself consisted of four nights of street fighting in New York City's Greenwich Village, sparked by a routine police raid on the Stonewall Inn, a popular gay bar. The New York Times' account following the first night's events was titled "4 Policemen Hurt in 'Village' Raid" and read in part:

> Hundreds of young men went on a rampage in Greenwich Village shortly after 3 A.M. yesterday after a force of plainclothes men raided a bar that the police said was well known for its homosexual clientele. Thirteen persons were arrested and four policemen injured. ...
>
> The raid was one of three held on Village bars in the last two weeks, Inspector Pine said....
>
> Charges against the 13 who were arrested ranged from harassment and resisting arrest to disorderly conduct. A patrolman suffered a broken wrist, the police said.
>
> Throngs of young men congregated outside the inn last night, reading aloud condemnations of the police.

Although the Times' account was brief and didn't mention the leading role in the rebellion played by lesbians and male transvestites and Black and Latin participants, it was probably more than the Times or any other newspaper had written about gay people since the anti-gay hysteria in Boise 14 years earlier.

The social context within which the new movement arose was a highly explosive one. A youth rebellion of wide scope and international significance that had as its primary focus the Vietnam war was in full swing at the time. The continuing war against Black America was also being challenged, especially by the Black Panthers, who were at the height of their influence in 1969, 1970 and 1971. The Students for a Democratic Society was also at the peak of its size and power in 1969. Awareness of women's special oppression was spreading rapidly and organizations to fight for women's rights were springing up everywhere. Demonstrations against racism and U.S. imperialism were frequent and involved hundreds of thousands of people in every part of the country.

## Vietnam—An Inspiration to All the Oppressed

On the international level it was, of course, Vietnam that dominated the thoughts of millions. The inspiring example of the Vietnamese liberation fighters and the success of the Tet Offensive opened many eyes to the Pentagon's lies and to the power of an oppressed people united by their struggle for freedom. To a lesser but still important extent the French students' and workers' revolt of May 1968 did likewise. A third important international factor was the revolutionary foreign policy that Peoples China was pursuing in that period. Many Black people and many students developed a serious interest in the political thought of Marx, Lenin, Trotsky, Che, Ho Chi Minh, Mao and other great revolutionaries in this period. The pacifist misleaders and the liberal bourgeois politicians were very much on the defensive.

Born as it was in the flames of struggle, the lesbian and gay liberation movement was predominantly activist in its first stages. For example, in New York City in late 1969 and 1970, there was a whole series of demonstrations against continuing police harassment of gay bars. In one incident in March 1970 the arrest of 166 people in a Greenwich Village gay bar precipitated a militant, angry march of 500 the following night. In May an organization of Third World gays, the Third World Gay Revolution, was formed. Among the organizers of this group were leaders of the 1968 Columbia University rebellion and others who had participated in the armed takeover of Cornell University. In June 5,000 gays marched to honor the first anniversary of the Stonewall Rebellion.

In August 1970, a struggle erupted at New York University over the use of university facilities by lesbian and gay students. At the end of August, 1,000 gay demonstrators protesting continuing police harassment clashed with police who were in the process of destroying a gay afterhours hangout in Greenwich Village. Inspired by the struggle going on in the streets below them, the women prisoners in the Village House of Detention began a rebellion of their own.

Other gay demonstrations were held against the police, against the imprisonment of lesbian and gay people, against the use of shock treatment to "cure" gays at Bellevue Hospital, against the Catholic Church, against bourgeois politicians and against the biased portrayals of lesbian, gay and transgendered people in the bourgeois media. In both New York City and San Francisco there were several important struggles at this time against the firings of gay workers. Also in San Francisco the annual convention of the American Psychiatric Association in June of 1970 was attacked by lesbian and gay activists demanding an end to the pseudo-scientific position of the medical profession on the issue of homosexuality.

At about the same time a struggle was organized against Macy's department store in San Francisco, which had stepped up entrapment of gay men in its restrooms. In December another struggle broke out in San Francisco when police attacked young men standing in front of a gay bar and seriously wounded one of them. Similar struggles occurred during this period in many other U.S. cities. In addition, lesbians and gay men by the hundreds and thousands worked to free Angela Davis, Ruchell Magee, the many Panther political prisoners, the Soledad Brothers, and to end the Vietnam War.

The Panthers' Revolutionary Peoples' Constitutional Convention in September of 1970 was certainly one of the most electrifying events of this period, and gay participation in it was strong. Though there were many difficulties, both the lesbians and gay men at this Convention showed strong support for the Panthers, who were at that time being hit by a murderous assault in city after city directed from the highest offices of the Nixon regime.

## A New Period of Class Struggle Is Opening

But you only have to think back to this period of strongest lesbian and gay upsurge to see that we face a very different situation today. Defeated in Southeast Asia, U.S. imperialism has begun a new war—against the living standards of the working people here at home. There is an historic struggle, a reviving class struggle, looming in the U.S. today. Lesbian and gay people, who have been in the front ranks of the movement for Black civil rights, who fought by the thousands against the Vietnam war, who have taken up the struggle for their own liberation—gay people will be leaders in the struggle for socialism also.

We have attempted to show in this book that the oppression of lesbian, gay and transgendered people, like the oppression of women, is historically rooted in material factors accompanying the rise of class society. Sexual oppression has grown and flourished, in spite of its harm to the masses of people, because it serves an important function for the class that rules. Lesbians and gays, therefore, like all women, like the victims of racism and national chauvinism, have a special interest in overthrowing capitalism.

It is, of course, impossible to know in any concrete way what the lives of human beings will be like in the communist future, when the systems of exploitation and oppression have finally been ended, when racism and sexism no longer exist, when national boundaries have disappeared, and when money and all the other strange artifacts of class society have been consigned to the museums.

What kind of human relationships will develop? How will people love? These are not burning questions that demand immediate and detailed answers and, in fact, such answers are not possible. Marxism is a potent tool in the struggle for a better world, but it is not a crystal ball. Yet Marxists are concerned with the questions of love and sexuality. We are confident that with the end of exploitation and oppression will come the possibility of much fuller, richer and more profound human relationships. Here is the way Workers World Party leader Dorothy Ballan puts it in her book *Feminism and Marxism:* "On the question of love, Marxists seek to focus not on "free love" but on how to set love free, that is, to emancipate love from the outmoded, artificial social restraints which are the heritage of social systems based on class domination and class oppression."

For the capitalist class, each passing day deepens the dread and gloom as their system grows weaker and weaker and the socialist countries grow stronger and stronger. For revolutionaries, the future is bright. Yet it cannot be denied that there is a lingering doubt in the minds of many progressive lesbians and gays. The socialist countries and left parties seem to be almost as prejudiced toward gay people as the capitalists are. Will this continue to be the case?

In the dynamic atmosphere of struggle and change that accompanied the first wave of gay liberation, lesbian and gay people were generally well received. What resistance there was tended to be shortlived. Huey Newton's historic statement in support of gay liberation, shortly after the nationwide movement freed him from prison in August, 1970, went a long way toward breaking down homophobia in the ranks of progressive youths, both Black and white. On the other hand, the leaders of the RYM II faction of SDS, who were at that time laying the groundwork for what were later to become the rival "Maoist" groups the October League and the Revolutionary Union, remained insensitive on the issue of lesbian and gay oppression and ultimately developed political positions hostile to gay people.

The U.S. Communist Party and the Progressive Labor Party also confronted the new-born gay liberation movement with hostility. The Communist Party actually tried to bar gay people from a number of demonstrations in support of Angela Davis. Nor has the Socialist Workers Party, a reformist grouping that calls itself Trotskyist, shown consistent support for lesbian and gay people. Before they began giving lip service to gay civil rights in the early 1970s, they actually had a policy of excluding lesbian and gay people from membership in their organization.

In reacting in such a prejudiced manner, these groups, while calling themselves communist, were and are doing no more than exhibiting the standard bourgeois prejudices against homosexuality. They have felt, consciously or otherwise, the ideological power the imperialist ruling class still possesses in its period of decline, and they have buckled under to it on the lesbian and gay question as they have on many other important political questions.

It is hard, but absolutely necessary, to challenge bourgeois authority on every issue. The eyes of the billionaires are blinded by greed, racism, sexism, homophobia, and the self-indulgent fantasy that their system will last forever. Aspiring leaders of the oppressed and working people are obligated to provide an objective alternative to the distorted, pessimistic and erroneous views with which the bosses still try to cloud and poison the minds of poor and working people.

Sam Marcy, the chairperson of Workers World Party, a multinational Communist organization that has a proud record of support for the struggle of lesbian, gay and transgendered people, put forth the following ideas on this issue at the 1972 national conference of the Party, barely three years after Stonewall:

Our first, most elementary and fundamental duty as well as objective on this question, is to completely eliminate and abolish all forms of persecution and oppression of gay people. We must also fight against all ideological, political, and social manifestations of gay oppression which may be reflected in our own ranks.

We must remember that the worldwide impact of the reaction that followed in the Soviet Union after Stalin took over had tremendous repercussions in all the countries of the world. When Stalin decided in 1934 to jail homosexuals on some pretext, on grounds which differed little from infractions of bourgeois laws against homosexuals, he signaled a turn in what was, broadly speaking, the vanguard elements of the progressive elements of the world.

To this day, if there is little support or sympathy in the revisionist Communist Parties of the world for gay people, it is in no small measure due to the reactionary position taken by Stalin in the early 1930s, and continued to this day in the Soviet Union. It made the formidable obstacles in the way of gay people becoming liberated heavier rather than lighter. For if the advanced guard, the most enlightened section of the progressive people, takes a turn to the right, it bodes ill for all other segments of the oppressed people. ...

The socialist revolution is a permanent revolution, one of continuous change. Along with many changes that need to be made in the socialist countries, the gay question is surely one of them. In the meantime, we ought to concentrate on preparing our own revolution, in which the struggle for the liberation of all oppressed people, including gay people, is an indispensible condition for victory.

# Afterword:
# The Struggle Continues

"In the meantime, we ought to concentrate on preparing our own revolution, in which the struggle for the liberation of all oppressed people, including gay people, is an indispensable condition for victory."

More than two decades later, Sam Marcy's prescription for overturning lesbian and gay oppression is more valid than ever. But the road isn't easy. The ruling class blocks the way at every juncture. In the years since the original publication of this book the path has proved to be full of twists and turns.

## Fighting on many fronts

The setbacks to socialism, the successful invasions of Grenada, Panama and Iraq, and the long period of the right-wing offensive at home have emboldened the U.S. ruling class. But at the same time it has been made desperate by its inability to solve the inherent contradictions of capitalism and make the economy work. As a result of both this confidence and insecurity the bourgeoisie and its government have launched direct attacks against oppressed groups, chipping away at rights won through earlier struggles.

Thus, affirmative action to redress centuries of racism is targeted; women's reproductive freedom and the right to choose abortion are narrowed; Nazi and Klan groupings are permitted to organize openly; the religious right wing is encouraged to mount local and statewide campaigns against lesbian and gay civil rights. At the same time the ruling class fashions scapegoats out of vulnerable groups—like immigrant workers, or people with AIDS, or transgendered people—and tries to coax the rest of the working class into blaming them for the heightening crisis of unemployment, hunger, homelessness, lack of health care, and so on.

This tactic works less and less. Probably the most heartening occurrence in the years since this book was written is the real advances made toward strengthening class solidarity among lesbians, gay men and heterosexuals. A May 1981 march on the Pentagon against U.S. intervention in El Salvador became the first national anti-war event at which an open representative of the lesbian/gay community spoke. Increasingly from then on, that was more the rule than the exception. The bosses can no longer count on gay-baiting as a sure thing to throw a union organizing drive into disarray. Out-of-the-closet lesbians and gays are active in the anti-racist struggle and on every other front. With their energy and commitment to the overall struggle they have won the allegiance of many of their class sisters and brothers.

The first national lesbian and gay rights march on Washington took place in October 1979. It was big—some quarter-million people—and bold and exciting. There was a splendid turnout from the gay community. But few straight supporters were in evidence. The second national march on Washington for lesbian and gay rights drew over half-a-million people in October 1987. This time there were many straight supporters, including members of groups like Parents and Friends of Lesbians and Gays and, significantly, a contingent of union members. A historic labor/gay rights solidarity reception took place at the AFL-CIO headquarters the day before. Plans for the third national march, on April 25, 1993, included a much bigger labor contingent, along with other progressive groups. The NAACP was among the march's first endorsers.

The organized left wing, although considerably diminished as a result of the setbacks in the socialist countries, has progressed on the issue. The Communist Party USA finally dropped its backward anti-gay position at the end of the 1980s. The Socialist Workers Party still officially supports the struggle, although it has not actually taken part in the lesbian and gay movement since the early 1970s.

Workers World Party has been an active participant since the start of the modern movement for lesbian and gay liberation. Even before the formation of the Gay Caucus of WWP's youth group, Youth Against War & Fascism, in 1971, our gay and straight comrades were actively supporting the struggle against lesbian and gay oppression. We didn't need a formal position paper to have it made clear to us that lesbian, gay and transgendered people were oppressed and that their struggle should be supported. Nevertheless, it was—and is—important to bring communist understanding to every social phenomenon and class consciousness to every struggle. Publishing this book was part of WWP's effort to do so.

Over the years, WWP members, led by its large lesbian and gay caucus, have fought in cities across the country on many fronts: blocking filming of the anti-gay movie *Cruising*; demonstrating against FDA policies on AIDS; protesting in San Francisco when the assassin of openly gay City Supervisor Harvey Milk was let out of prison after a light sentence; marching against Reaganite anti-gay legislation; taking the streets in front of the New York Stock Exchange with ACT UP to protest drug company profiteering; denouncing the Supreme Court's Hardwick decision upholding "sodomy" laws; organizing against the Nazi David Duke's gubernatorial campaign in Louisiana; mobilizing against gay bashers; demonstrating at Republican and Democratic Conventions; speaking and marching at Lesbian and Gay Pride rallies; standing in solidarity with the transgender struggle; organizing gay trade unionists. Other than the lesbian and gay press, which has multiplied over the years, Workers World weekly newspaper has provided the most consistent coverage of the gay struggle in this country.

There have been many fronts to that struggle, as the movement has stretched and matured. Organizations of gay and lesbian people of color flourish in every major city. The struggle against racism is recognized as an essential element of the lesbian and gay movement. New demands, like "domestic partner" rights to put lesbian and gay families on a more equal footing with those based on heterosexual marriage, have issued forth even as the struggle for basic civil rights and a national gay rights law continues. There are lesbian and gay student organizations on most campuses, and at least one public school system, New York City's, boasts a special high school for lesbian and gay youths—the Harvey Milk School—where they are provided a haven from persecution and harassment and offered respect and love. A movement for transgender liberation has emerged, and is growing swiftly.

The type of anti-gay violence to which McCubbin refers in reporting several early-1970s incidents continues. In fact, it seems to have increased, prompted and encouraged by reactionaries in power and by the religious right. Now, however, self-defense groups patrol gay neighborhoods and monitor police brutality. Lesbian mothers must still fight in some places for custody of their children, but in other venues lesbians and gay men are now accepted as adoptive parents.

AIDS has been the community's common denominator since 1981. The scope of the tragedy cannot be exaggerated. By the start of 1993, it had killed at least 165,000 people in the U.S. It has cut a bitter swath across the entire multinational gay community, hitting African Americans and Latinos disproportionately. That pattern holds true among heterosexuals with AIDS, too. From the start, the right wing seized on this disease as if it were a gift from their gods. The government for the most part refused to mount a serious, all-out, fully funded program of research, treatment, education and prevention. Instead the epidemic was allowed to spread through the gay and Third World communities. People were left homeless, without health care. The pharmaceuticals industry first did nothing, then brazenly profiteered and manipulated the market, basing its testing and release of drugs on the bottom line. Meanwhile, reactionary elements were let loose, with a nod from the top, to try to manufacture an atmosphere of AIDS panic and discrimination.

In the context of the AIDS crisis in particular, the Catholic Church has carried on its reactionary role as outlined in this book. While most lay Catholics undoubtedly feel compassion for people with AIDS and are not consumed with homophobia, the Church officialdom has taken an aggressive anti-gay stand that AIDS activists rightly characterize as murderous. Pope John Paul II actually issued a statement essentially blaming gay men for AIDS. In the U.S., some European countries, Africa, the Philippines and elsewhere, the Church has opposed and tried to block the distribution of condoms, both among the populace at large and to high-school students in particular. Some in the Church hierarchy, like New York's Cardinal John O'Connor, have carved out a special niche for themselves as anti-gay zealots.

None of it—neither the virus nor the virulent bigots—has held back the struggle. In fact, the emergence of the AIDS movement, painful as the need for it was, broadened and deepened the lesbian and gay movement. It brought to the fore a new layer of activists tempered by this life-and-death struggle.

There's one other killer that deserves mention: the Pentagon. Over the years there was more and more outrage at the unrestrained discrimination, harassment and violence lesbians and gay men endured in the U.S. military. The conditions described in this book haven't changed at all. Lesbians, especially, face the constant threat of witch hunts. They are discharged at more than double the rate of gay men. But something did change: People started fighting back, inside and outside the armed forces. In several highly publicized cases, GIs discharged from the military simply for being gay took the brass to court to challenge their ouster. At the same time, the movement started to take on the issue, demanding an end to the military's ban on openly gay or lesbian troops. It really took on steam at college campuses, where the 1980s and early 1990s saw a number of struggles over demands to bar military recruiters and ROTC as long as the anti-gay ban remained in effect. When the matter finally hit the front pages in the first days of the Clinton administration in 1993 and the joint chiefs of staff nearly staged a mutiny at the possibility that the president might sign an executive order lifting the ban, the importance of this struggle became clear.

The Pentagon is an inherently reactionary institution. The brass are stalwarts of racism, sexual harassment, and lesbian/gay oppression. Just as the U.S. military enforces imperialist expansion and exploitation abroad, it also serves a repressive function inside the U.S. The hierarchy depends on keeping the rank and file divided and subjugated. Anything that contributes to solidarity among the ranks constitutes a challenge to the officers—potentially, to their very right to issue orders. After all, most young people enlist because of an "economic draft"—there aren't any other decent jobs available. It's not patriotism or a desire to die fighting against Third World countries that drives most people into the armed forces—it's economic necessity. This is as true for lesbians and gays as straight GIs. Once the obstacles to solidarity among the ranks—racism, sexism, lesbian and gay oppression—are dissolved, the troops will be able to see that they have more in common with each other than with the generals and admirals who make their lives miserable. Such a state of affairs implies the potential for not only serious reforms, but eventually a revolutionary situation within the military at the point when a general upsurge erupts.

**Worldwide Scope**

Dramatic international developments have affected the lesbian and gay movement along with all other struggles. Sharp setbacks in the socialist countries were accompanied by a period of worldwide political reaction. A capitalist economic crisis, more profound and protracted than the previous cycles of boom and bust, has made life harder for workers and oppressed peoples everywhere. It prompted intensified aggression from the ruling class in the form of union busting, cutbacks, racism and racist violence, gay bashing and homophobia, and attacks on women's rights.

The U.S., although vanquished in Vietnam, has never let up on its worldwide program of intervention and war. Washington has funded repeated Israeli invasions of Lebanon, the contra war against Sandinista Nicaragua and the apartheid-backed UNITA mercenaries in Angola; invaded Grenada and Panama; mercilessly bombed Iraq; and occupied Somalia.

The ascendancy of counter-revolutionary forces in the former workers' states of Eastern Europe and the Soviet Union, although it will prove to be temporary in historical terms, removed a big brake on U.S. imperialism. Vietnam, China, north Korea and Cuba are in an increasingly defensive and isolated position.

The counter-revolutionary developments in the socialist countries have affected the lesbian and gay movement in several ways. Within the former workers' states themselves, Nazi elements that had been suppressed for four decades crawled out from under their rocks and indulged in racist, anti-Semitic and anti-gay terror sprees. In the former German Democratic Republic, in particular, the shift has been harsh. There, in the country where the lesbian and gay rights movement first started in the 19th century, great advances had been made throughout the 1970s and 1980s. Progressive changes in the educational curriculum meant East German schoolchildren were taught that homosexuality was a natural, healthy orientation. There were many gay clubs in cities like Berlin, and social attitudes toward gays and lesbians were improving, supported by the government. In the U.S. people with AIDS died homeless in the street, and lesbian and gay workers had to demand the right to include their lovers in their medical benefits. In the GDR, by contrast, there was housing for all, and universal, free health care meant equal benefit rights wasn't even an issue. Since the capitalist Federal Republic of Germany took control of the former GDR, all that has changed.

The setbacks have had repercussions elsewhere, too. In Nicaragua, President Daniel Ortega warmly endorsed the budding lesbian and gay movement that was part of the Sandinista movement. But since the right-wing UNO forces took over the government in 1990, these courageous activists have been under attack. Elsewhere in Latin America—especially Argentina, Brazil, Colombia and Chile, as well as in Mexico, where there is quite an active gay movement—the ruling class and land-owning aristocracy have unleashed harsh terror campaigns, including assassinations, against gays and transgendered people. The African National Congress of South Africa has taken a forthright position for lesbian and gay rights, while the racist apartheid regime continues to target Black gay activists for special violence. Repression has greeted the new gay and lesbian movements in India, Thailand and other Asian countries.

Both U.S. imperialism and the setbacks in the socialist camp are directly implicated in the difficulties the lesbian and gay communities in these Third World countries face.

The U.S. has continued to intervene against the oppressed around the world on behalf of the multinational corporations. Neocolonial exploitation creates poverty and despair in developing countries, and difficult conditions of life gave rise to many anti-imperialist struggles. With the emergence of these mass movements the lesbian and gay community, in turn, has become politically activated in many countries. But the struggle is very hard, especially now. Before, the Soviet Union in particular helped strengthen the national liberation struggles with political support and material aid. This support may not have explicitly extended to the nascent gay movements in Third World countries; but the existence of the Soviet counterweight to the U.S. imperialist colossus implicitly strengthened the gay struggle along with other revolutionary currents. In the present period, by contrast, the progressive movement everywhere is under the gun, weakened by the collapse of the Soviet Union. This has necessarily created a tough situation for the lesbian and gay struggle, too. Despite these difficulties, though, the struggle continues on every continent. The fighters persevere.

Meanwhile, there is tremendous pressure on the small socialist country of Cuba, an island nation whose 10 million people have vowed to fight to the death to defend their right to self-determination. Three decades of the U.S. blockade against that country, combined with the loss of material and economic support from the former Soviet Union, have created terrible hardship. Continuous U.S. threats and belligerence force the Cuban people to expend precious energy and resources on self-defense.

Fortunately, one cynical facet of the U.S. campaign against socialist Cuba is losing its punch. Beginning in the mid-to-late 1970s, a propaganda campaign meant to turn the U.S. lesbian and gay community against Cuba was mounted. Some influential gay writers took up the crusade against Cuba as their special cause. But there can be no doubt that the campaign itself emanated from the highest levels of the U.S. government, where disinformation experts have honed their skills for decades. Unfortunately, many well-meaning people were taken in. Most never stopped to wonder why the U.S. ruling class—the greatest bastion of homophobia, bigotry and AIDS-based bias in the world, the main source of lesbian and gay oppression—suddenly cared about gay people in Cuba. They didn't realize they were being used as pawns in a dual effort to break down solidarity with the people of Cuba and redirect the gay community's anger away from the real source of oppression—the U.S. ruling class and its government.

In Cuba as elsewhere, capitalism had given rise to homophobia. The Cuban Revolution inherited a set of social conditions and attitudes left over from centuries of colonialism and neocolonialism—that is, from capitalism—and from the influence of the Catholic Church brought to the island by the Spanish invaders. Homophobia, like racism, the subjugation of women and prostitution was a remnant of capitalism, not a creation of socialism. In fact, because bigotry hurt the revolutionary effort, socialism provided the avenue for its demise.

Anti-gay violence is extremely rare in Cuba, unlike the U.S. In 1986 the revolutionary government revised the penal code, striking all anti-gay laws left over from the Batista era. An official program educates the populace about same-sex love as a normal variant of human behavior. The demographics of AIDS are different in Cuba than in this country. Gay men do not make up the majority of cases. So it's not accurate to characterize public health policy as tainted by discrimination.

Lesbians, gays and people with AIDS continue to be active participants in the revolutionary transformation of Cuban society. And happily, the U.S. ruling class's lock on the lesbian and gay community as an ally against Cuba is disintegrating. The AIDS movement, impressed by the quality of Cuban medical care, free and available to all, has for the most part dropped its hostility, properly concentrating its ire on this country's rulers. More and more lesbians and gay men are leaders in the Cuba solidarity movement; there is now a group called Queers For Cuba.

## Warriors for Human Liberation

The years have confirmed this book's perspective on the meaning of capitalism for lesbian, gay and transgendered people. Class antagonisms have, if anything, heightened. The class struggle is sharpening. For now, the combatants on the other side of the trenches—the ruling class—are much more acutely aware of this than most of us are. But that is likely to change. And sooner rather than later.

The lesbian and gay struggle in the U.S. has grown exponentially since Stonewall. It is a multinational movement that has taken as its symbols the rainbow flag representing diversity and unity, and the pink triangle of the Nazi concentration camps. Like every movement it has also inevitably spawned its share of moderates, careerists, politicians and so on. The liberal bourgeoisie tends to look to these elements as representatives of the community. In reality, however, the lesbian and gay community is made up primarily of workers and oppressed people. That's why the movement has successfully retained an edge of fury and militancy in the midst of a period of deep reaction. Young, working-class lesbians and gays continually revitalize and renew the struggle, bringing an ever deeper tinge of radicalism to what is at its core an extremely radical movement.

As the 20th century draws to a close an era of renewed, reinvigorated struggles is on the horizon. The class barricades will be erected again, in the U.S. and around the world. When that happens, the lesbian and gay movement can be expected to take another sharp turn to the left. Lesbians, gay men and transgendered people will stand tall in the revolutionary army of workers, the poor and oppressed as full partners—proud, equal, angry warriors for the cause of human liberation.

Shelley Ettinger

## AUTHOR'S NOTE

As I wondered what would be an appropriate message for this space, my thoughts kept turning to the young lesbians, gay men and transgendered people who are out on the streets today, fighting for the future. If this book adds something to your sense of personal identity and pride, if it deepens your historical perspective, if it helps you in your search for the source of social injustice, or if it strengthens your determination to fight that injustice, that's great. That's why the book was originally written. That's why it's being re-released.

Of course, since the book's first appearance much more material that is relevant to the ideas presented here has come to light. Were the resources and time available, it would be good to enrich and strengthen this work with them. But the war of ideas that must be waged with the capitalist ruling class, as important as it is, is not all that needs doing.

In fact, when you think about all that needs to be done, the enormity of it seems like enough to stop anyone cold. Before you let that happen to you, consider this. There is a way to tackle all the tasks, to fight on all the fronts at the same time—and to do it well, with absolute confidence that these efforts are all contributing to our eventual triumph over the world's exploiters and oppressors.

I'm referring here to the kind of organization that has been developed on the basis of the whole historical experience of working people and the oppressed the world over. It's been tested over and over. It works. It's a revolutionary-struggle organization whose purpose is to end all class exploitation and oppression through mass struggle.

In the United States, Workers World Party is this kind of organization. Maybe you already know something about this party. Party members and friends are active in struggles of all kinds. The party newspaper, *Workers World*, reports these struggles and analyzes national and international events. If you like this book, you should subscribe to this weekly newspaper. You should also get in touch with the Workers World Party branch in your area, come to meetings and participate in activities.

So join us! The struggle continues!

Bob McCubbin<br>February 1993

# Selected Bibliography

Ballan, Dorothy, *Feminism and Marxism.* New York: World View Publishers, 1971.

Bentley, Eric, *Lord Alfred's Lover: A Play.* Toronto: Personal Library, 1981.

Cant, Bob and Susan Hemmings, Eds., *Radical Records: Thirty Years of Lesbian and Gay History, 1957-1987.* London: Routledge, 1988.

Duberman, Martin, Martha Vicinus & George Chauncey Jr., Eds., *Hidden From History: Reclaiming the Gay and Lesbian Past.* New York: New American Library, 1989.

Duberman, Martin, *About Time: Exploring the Gay Past.* New York: Gay Presses of New York City, 1986.

Engels, Frederick, *The Origin of the Family, Private Property and the State.* New York: International Publishers, 1972.

Feinberg, Leslie, *Transgender Liberation: A Movement Whose Time Has Come.* New York: WW Publishers, 1992.

Ford, Clellan Stearns, *Patterns of Sexual Behavior.* New York: Harper and Row, 1951.

Frazer, James, *The Golden Bough.* New York: New American Library, 1964.

Gay American Indians, *Living the Spirit: A Gay American Indian Anthology.* New York: St. Martins, 1988.

Gerassi, John, *The Boys of Boise: Furor, Vice and Folly in an American City.* New York: MacMillan, 1966.

Gimbutas, Marija, *The Civilization of the Goddess.* San Francisco: Harper, 1991.

Gimbutas, Marija, *The Language of the Goddess: Unearthing the Hidden Symbols of Western Civilization.* San Francisco: Harper & Row, 1989.

Grahn, Judy, *Another Mother Tongue: Gay Words, Gay Worlds.* Boston: Beacon Press, 1984.

Heger, Heinz, *The Men with the Pink Triangle.* London: Gay Men's Press, 1980.

Katz, Jonathan, *Gay American History.* New York: Crowell, 1976.

Kautsky, Karl, *Foundations of Christianity,* New York: Monthly Review Press, 1972.

Lauritsen, John and David Thorstad, *The Early Homosexual Rights Movement (1864-1935)*. New York: Times Change Press, 1974.

Lenin, V.I., *The State and Revolution*. Beijing: Foreign Languages Press, 1965.

Levi-Strauss, Claude, *Tristes Tropiques*. New York: Criterion, 1961.

Martin, Del and Phyllis Lyon, *Lesbian/Woman*. San Francisco: Glide Publications, 1972.

Martin, M. Kay and Barbara Voorhies, *Female of the Species*. New York: Columbia University Press, 1975.

Marx, Karl and Frederick Engels, *Manifesto of the Communist Party*. Beijing: Foreign Languages Press, 1965.

Mead, Margaret, *Coming of Age in Samoa*. New York: Morrow, 1961.

Murphy, Lawrence R., *Perverts by Official Order: The Campaign Against Homosexuals by the United States Navy*. New York: Haworth Press, 1988.

Niethammer, Carolyn, *Daughters of the Earth—The Lives and Legends of American Indian Women*. New York: MacMillan, 1977.

Reed, Evelyn, *Woman's Evolution—From Matriarchal Clan to Patriarchal Family*. New York: Pathfinder Press, 1975.

Reich, Wilhelm, *The Sexual Revolution*. New York: Farrar, Straus & Giroux, 1969.

Schneebaum, Tobias, *Keep the River on Your Right*. New York: Grove, 1969.

Steakley, James, *The Homosexual Emancipation Movement in Germany*. New York: Arno Press, 1975.

Stone, Merlin, *When God Was a Woman*. New York: Harcourt Brace Jovanovich, 1976.

Timmons, Stuart, *The Trouble with Harry Hay: Founder of the Modern Gay Movement*. Boston: Alyson, 1990.

Trotsky, Leon, *Problems of Everyday Life*. New York: Pathfinder Press, 1973.

Weiss, Andrea, *Before Stonewall: The Making of a Gay and Lesbian Community*. Tallahassee, Fla.: Naiad Press, 1988.

Westermarck, Edward, *The Origin and Development of the Moral Ideas*. London: MacMillan, 1906.

Wilde, Oscar, *The Soul of Man Under Socialism*. New York: Humboldt, 1891.

Williams, Walter, *The Spirit and the Flesh*. New York: Putnam, 1988.